GENETIC RESOURCES

A Practical Guide to their Conservation

Daniel Querol

Zed Books Ltd
London and New Jersey

Third World Network
Penang, Malaysia

Genetic Resources is published by
Zed Books Ltd, 57 Caledonian Road, London N1 9BU, UK and
165 First Avenue, Atlantic Highlands, New Jersey 07716, USA,
and by Third World Network, 87, Cantonment Road, 10250
Penang, Malaysia.

Cover design by Andrew Corbett

A catalogue record for this book is available
from the British Library.
US CIP is available from the US Library of Congress

ISBN 1 85649 203 6 Hb
ISBN 1 85649 204 4 Pb

Printed by Jutaprint
54 Kajang Road, 10150 Penang, Malaysia

Hay, hermanos,
muchísimo que hacer.
CESAR VALLEJO

There is, brothers,
plenty to be done.

This book is dedicated to the peasants of Buenavista,
Río San Juan, Nicaragua Libre, and to the memory of
Nong Tudying, from BATUNA.

CONTENTS

LIST OF TABLES

LIST OF FIGURES

Some plants and their centers of origin
MESOAMERICA

Maize (*Zea mays*)

Gourds (*Cucurbita moshata*)

Chillies (*Capsicum annuum*)

Sisal (*Agave sisalana*)

Vanilla (*Vanilla fragrans*)

Cocoa (*Theobroma cacao*)

Anona (*Annona squamosa*)

Zapote (*Manilkara achras*)

SOUTHEAST ASIA

Winter cucumber (*Cucumis sp.*)

Nutmeg (*Myristica fragrans*)

Red ginger (*Zingiber officinale*)

Taro (*Colocasia esculenta*)

NORTHERN CHINA

Tangerine (*Citrus sp.*)

Tea (*Thea sinensis*)

Chinese medicinal plants

Kangkong (*Ipomoea aquatica*)

ANDEAN REGION

Potato (*Solanum tuberosum*)

Sweet potato (*Ipomoea batatas*)
(also from Central America)

Papaya (*Carica papaya*)
(also in Central America)

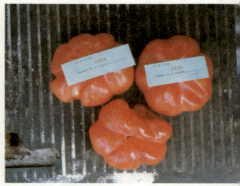

Tomato (*Lycopersicum esculentum*)

OTHER REGIONS

CLEOPATRA

Wheat (*Triticum aestivum*)
(From Central Asia and Middle east)

Pigeon pea   (*Cajanus cajan*)
(Africa and Mesoamerica)

Breadfruit tree (*Artocarpus altilis*)
(From Polynesia)

Safflower (*Carthamus tinctorius*)
(Middle East)

PREFACE

OUR TECHNOLOGICAL DEVELOPMENT must happen within a political and economic context. This book tries to be coherent with that principle. Presently, there is no text in Spanish (or in English) which describes the practical problems and possible solutions in the collection, conservation and use of our genetic resources. It is even more difficult to find a technical and economic framework on this subject, for Third World scientists and peasants. This book wants to fill that gap.

The first chapter describes some basic concepts and locates the subject in the living world. The second chapter presents the practical importance of genetic resources. The third chapter analyses the economic and political implications of genetic resources for Third World countries and the organizations which, on a national and international level, work on the subject. Chapters IV to VII describe the technical processes for the collection, conservation and study of genetic resources. As appendices, some practical information is given, including a glossary of terms.

This book was written by bits and pieces, over various years in our economically underdeveloped countries. It was initially structured as a manual for the "Genetic Resources and Genebanks" course in the Chapingo Autonomous University, in Mexico in 1984, where it was enriched with the help and ideas of colleagues from the Plant Science Department and the Regional Centers. Later, it was used in Nicaragua, as a discussion base for the creation of the Nicaraguan Genetic Resources Program, and practice, in the stimulating frame of a dynamic revolutionary process, eliminated the utopia and proved what could be fulfilled. Efforts over various years to establish a Genetic Resources Program in Peru allowed for long and fruitful discussions with peasants, technicians and scientists, who have to waste their energies — unfortunately — in the struggle against bureaucracy.

This book — maybe disordered, somehow outdated, with hard to find references and examples from everywhere — reflects the problems and advantages of scientific work in the Third World, where we must think and act simultaneously in many fields if we want to remain human.

ACKNOWLEDGMENTS

To the old friends in Indo-America who made the Spanish edition possible, specially Fidel Márquez, Miguel Holle and Paco Campodónico.

To the new friends in Malaysia
Martin Khor because he thought it was worth publishing
Linda Ooi for the typing
Chee Yoke Ling and Nora Syed Ibrahim for the editing
Lim Jee Yuan for the patience
Francis for the entertainment.
And to Sandrita Castrillo.

Traditional maize and bean varieties, hand planted and harvested. The leaves and the upper parts of the stems have been harvested (for fodder), in order to avoid casting shadows on the growing bean plants. The ear stays in the field to dry. When the beans grow, the stems of maize are used as support for the vines (Photo taken in Chiapas, Mexico, 10.1983).

I
Basic Concepts

TODAY, many people will have come across the term genetic resources. The term is vaguely defined: anything we can use as a resource for the present and the future which originates in the plant or animal kingdoms.

This ambiguity is largely due to the fact that systematic work on available genetic resources in nature is quite recent. Even though peasants have always worked with most of the species which surround them, scientists in this century have specialised in the use of a very limited part of the potential of plants and animals.

In this book we will try to clarify the concept of genetic resources in the plant kingdom and propose ways to collect and utilise those resources, thereby enlarging the range of crops and the variability within them.

1. GERMPLASM – GENETIC RESOURCES

From an etymological point of view, "germplasm" is a word with two roots: "germ" from the Latin "germen" which means the rudimentary principle of a new organic being and "plasma" from the Greek "plasma" which is defined as the form and in the widest sense, the undefined matter. Therefore, germplasm is the matter where one can find the principle which can grow and develop.

On the other hand, genetic resources can be defined as the goods or the potential means (the resource) which is found in genes (genetic). This expression is used when one is conscious of the economic value which these resources have, as one does with other resources (forest, minerals, energy, etc.).

Genetic resources are understood as the genetic variability stored in the chromosomes and in other structures containing deoxyribonucleic acid (DNA, molecules which constitute the genes) which codify the development of polypeptide chains (proteins). These polypeptides determine the functioning of the living organism in which they are found, as well as its basic functions (respiration, photosynthesis, and nutrient absorption in the case of plants) and also its specific characteristics like taste, resistance to diseases and pests, or the colour of the fruits.

The term germplasm, which came before the concept of genetic resources, was proposed by Weissmann at the end of the last century, to differentiate the parts of the plants with a reproductive capacity from those which had only a vegetative function. The term germplasm has a technical connotation, without any reference to the economic and political importance of the same.

The term genetic resources appeared in the middle of this century, when efforts were made to define the potential for development of countries as related to their resources. The value of germplasm as a resource implies the understanding and consciousness of its practical importance.

Once germplasm is understood as one of the resources on which a country can count, political interests start to examine how it can be utilised. This is the origin of some of the most difficult discussions to be resolved satisfactorily as the problem is often tackled as a technical or economic one, even though it is essentially a question of political power: the country with political power can use the economic resource.

Genetic variability cannot be found uniformly distributed for all crops and over the whole surface of the earth. Vavilov (1935) and later Harlan (1971) described the centres of origin variability for many of the crops we presently use. These centres correspond almost always to places in which cultures flourished when Europe and North America were still woods and steppes with primitive hunters. In these centres of ancient cultures the inhabitants domesticated plants which at the time were still growing wild, selecting and breeding them according to their needs. Thus, we have wheat from Mesopotamia, beans from the Mayas, rice from the Chinese and mango from the Hindus. Practically all crops originated in the inter-tropical band from 35 degrees latitude North to 35 degrees latitude South, the band which did not freeze during the prehistoric glacial periods.

Practically all centres of origin are therefore in countries which are presently termed "underdeveloped". Hence, genetic variability, genetic resources, are to be found there. Historically, since the expansion of the colonial empires, the guidelines for research and the definition of work have been made in the central countries. One of the definitions of great importance for this subject is that genetic resources, as opposed to all other resources, should not be the patrimony of the countries in which they are to be found, but that they are the patrimony of humanity: there is no owner who can claim rights over them.

Mooney (1983) presents an example of the historical effects. Brazil, at the end of the last century, controlled 95% of the world's export of rubber from the trees of *Hevea brasiliensis*. For reason of scientific interest, according to them, English botanists illegally took germplasm for study at the Royal Botanical Gardens at Kew. A few years later, British colonies such as Sri Lanka, Singapore and Malaya (now Malaysia) had plantations of *Hevea brasiliensis* which reduced the Brazilian industry to 5% of the market, with the subsequent social crisis in Brazil. What was stolen from Brazil was not just germplasm: a genetic resource was stolen.

Even though Cristobal Colon took maize and beans to Europe since his first trip, the Spaniards did not have the clarity of the Englishmen about the potential utilisation of plants, as their objectives were centred in the gold and silver, even though they were zealous with quinine.

The value of genetic resources, beyond their importance for the culture and history of the country, resides in their economic effects on agriculture. It is difficult to propose a figure as to the contribution of germplasm to the value of modern agricultural production, as it depends to a large extent on the value one assigns to the raw material, the work of the old breeders and the modern ones, and to the production techniques. On the other hand, as well as for any other resource, it is important to differentiate its potential form (minerals in the mountains or plants on the mountains) from its final form of expression (metal bars or plant varieties resistant to diseases), and one must realize that the passage from one shape to the other is very often only achieved many years after the initial investment of effort and money, unless a research infrastructure pre-exists.

While reviewing a textbook on plant breeding by Poehlman (1965), it is easy to see the needs and use which were made of the genetic resources for all and every one of the crops planted in the United States. The global value of all these is difficult to determine. As an alternative, one can have a look at the specific value in certain cases:

The "discovery" of perennial teozintle (*Zea diploperennis*) in a farm of a Mexican peasant whose name has not been reported, could mean savings of US$4.4 billion a year in seeds for farmers in the United States, according to the estimate of an agronomist from the University of California at Berkeley (Witt, 1985). Teozintle is a plant closely related to maize, which grows after harvesting, without the need to replant.

The introduction of genes for resistance to pests and diseases in tomatoes and other vegetables, starting with "primitive" germplasm from Peru, Ecuador, Chile and Bolivia, is a routine procedure, indispensable for the survival of the industry of those crops in industrialized countries.

Alfalfa collected at the end of the 1970s, partially without the agreement of Libya, in Libyan territory, has been considered to be worth millions of dollars for the cattle industry in Australia (Mooney, 1983).

Wheat collected in Turkey in 1948 has avoided losses of approximately US$3 million a year, which were caused by wheat rust in the North West of the United States (Mooney, 1984).

The introduction of resistance to *Phytophtora sp.* from

"primitive" potatoes collected around the Titicaca Lake, to Dutch potatoes, avoided losses of millions of dollars every year to the seed industry of that country (Carlos Ochoa, Personal Communication).

In the examples mentioned before, the genetic resources have been utilised mainly in industrialised countries, and those countries have obtained profits which they consider "fair and legal". In most cases, the benefit does not accrue to the countries which supplied the resources in the first place.

2. EVOLUTION AND VARIABILITY OF SPECIES

Nowadays, few people will still continue considering the bible as a source of scientific information. Therefore, it is almost unnecessary to show that the species we currently know were not created in six days; Linnaeus however, still believed in the only act of creation.

Buffon in 1760, and Lamarcke in 1809, stated for the first time the theory of evolution which became a universal acceptance as it was widely documented and developed by Darwin in 1859. After many further contributions over the last decades, one of the models of evolution is the one proposed by Grant (1963), according to which evolution is the process which can be presented in the following manner:

Figure I.1   MODEL OF THE EVOLUTION PROPOSED BY GRANT IN 1963

Changes in the environment of the species
↓   ↓   ↓
Phenotypic adaptation (survival)
↓
Mutations (micromutations)
↓   ↓   ↓
Selection of this genotypes
↓
Evolved species

An example based on Figure I.1 can be given: a volcano erupts in an area where certain species exist in balance with the environment. The hot volcanic ashes burn the largest part of the plants and the remaining ones have to survive in a soil which is more acidic than the original one. Those plants which have well-developed roots or other visible (phenotypic) characteristics which allow them to resist will survive. During the following generations, the plants in which micromutations occur (which generally do occur) which increase their tolerance to acidity in the soil, will have better possibilities to establish in the new environment. An evolved species will have appeared.

This process is very slow. The adaptation is seldom visible and the favourable micromutation almost never. Considering the time span in which these changes occur, it is not difficult to accept this theory.

As an exercise to see the consistency of a model of evolution as was mentioned, it is possible to calculate the number of mutations which could have accumulated since the appearance of vascular plants on earth.

The first vascular plants appeared approximately 405 million years ago, at the beginning of the Devonian period during the Paleozoic period. The following plants, on which this book centres, originated at the beginning of the Cretaceous period, 135 million years ago (Grant, 1963). The species which presently exist on earth appeared approximately 80,000 years ago.

For example the gene "**sh**", which determines the shape of the seed of maize, has a frequency of mutation of one in a million (Dobzhansky, 1937). This mutation occurs every time pollen or egg cell is produced (meiosis - gamete formation). If we make the following assumptions:

a) Plants have an average of 10,000 genes.
b) Every gene has the same mutation frequency.
c) No reverse mutations occur
d) Each plant has had one reproductive cycle per year over 400 million years.

We would obtain

$$N = 10^4 \text{ genes} \times 10^{-6} \text{ mutations} \times (4 \times 10^8) \text{ cycles}$$

$$= 4 \times 10^6 \text{ accummulative mutations}$$

This means that if since the origin of the first vascular plants until today, there would have been only one plant which every year would have produced one plant as an offspring, there would have been 4 million mutations, enough to create 400 totally different species, each one with 10,000 genes. None of these species would have even one allele in common with one of the other species. The real figure of accumulative mutations is much larger, as there is not only one plant in the world at every cycle, but thousands of millions of plants.

2.1 Speciation, Taxonomy

If we observe the similarity of certain species (Figure I.2) from a phylogenetic point of view, it is necessary to study the evolutionary processes to understand the reasons for this resemblance.

A species in natural balanced conditions and with no problems with its environment, will automatically eliminate mutations which will not be useful for it, by the means of natural selection. If this species is found in a changing environment, it will need to adapt in order to survive. This adaptation can happen in different ways. The first and essential one, mutations and adaptations, was already discussed. Other means are:

a) Flow of genetic material (often pollen) from the outside.

The alleles can be from another species or from other races of the same species. Their presence will lead to recombinations and selections which can lead to the formation of new species.

b) Genetic drift

When the size of the population is reduced by some

Table I.1 Example of dichotomic classifications.
Classification according to Muller (1969).

PLANT KINGDOM
DIVISION Anthropyta
CLASS   Dicotyledons
FAMILY   Leguminosae
   Genus   *Vicia*
   Species   *V. sativa*   Wild
   Species   *V. faba*   Broad Bean, cultivated
   Species   *V. sativa*   Weed

   Genus *Phaseolus* (180 Species)
   Species   *P. obvallatus*   Wild
   Species   *P. artropurpureus*   Wild
   Species   *P. coccineous*   Scarlet Runner Bean
   Species   *P. vulgaris*   Bean, cultivated

FAMILY Amaranthaceae
   Genus *Amaranthus*
   Species   *A. hybridus*   Weed
   Species   *A. paniculatus*   Cultivated grain in America
   Species   *A. hybridus*   Vegetable in India
   Genus *Gomphrena*
   Species   *G. decumbens*   Wild
   Species   *G. globosa*   Virus indicator plant for
                                       potato

FAMILY Solanaceae
   Genus *Solanum*
   Species   *S. cervantesii*   Poisonous weed
   Species   *S. demisum*   Wild
   Species   *S. nigrum*   Medicinal
   Species   *S. tuberosum*   Cultivated potato
   Species   *S. andigena*   South American cultivated
                                         potato

   Genus *Physalis*
   Species *P. acuminata*   Wild skin-tomato
   Species *P. foetens*   Weed
   Species *P. molis*   Wild

external cause, certain low frequency alleles will be randomly eliminated. This will change the genetic constitution of the species.

c) Selection

Certain alleles can have a phenotypic expression which leads to the extinction of the carriers of these due to the pressure of selection in a changing environment.

All these factors intervene, having as an effect the transformation of the species. The consequences of this transformation are of two possible kinds. If the transformation happens for the whole species, the consequence is the evolution of the species, but if only a part of the species is affected, we observe differentiation, the subspeciation and eventually the appearance of a new species. This can be called divergent evolution.

Dobzhansky (1973) defines this differentiation according to its causes and establishes the term **"ecological race"** if the differences within the species are due to an adaptive distance; **"geographical race"** if these differences are due to physical distances and parallel evolution. This diverging process continues very often and leads to the development and evolution of new species.

With enough time (and nature has had it), the species continues evolving and diverting. Returning to Table I.1, we observe that within the family of the legumes, the genus *Phaseolus* has gone through an intense process of differentiation. However, the process is never finished. If we consider the term species from a strict point of view (populations which cross within themselves, producing fertile progenies, but which do not produce them when they cross with another population under natural conditions), even though they are classified as different species, *Phaseolus coccineous* when pollinated with *Phaseolus vulgaris* produces fertile and vigorous seeds for the first generation (F1). Differences in many characters are marked; however, the characteristic utilised for the taxonomic classification is not completely correct.

Therefore, one can talk of taxonomic species for the

general classification work; but as we know, in reality there is a graduation which goes from the identity, in the case of plants of vegetative reproduction, passing through similar races and symmetric species and arrives all the way to the real biological species.

Today, as a consequence of this process of diverging evolution, there are 1.5 million species of living organisms described (Grant, 1963). Of these, 328,300 are plant species, 286,000 of which are flowering plants. Every year, approximately 4,800 more species are being described. In 1987, there must be at least 400,000 species of flowering plants described and many more are still to be described; especially tropical species. It would not be excessive to consider that on the earth, there are approximately 500,000 flowering plant species.

In the case of genetic resources, it is not enough to collect one sample of the studied species, but one has to look at the variability between races, ecotypes and genotypes. In the case of wheat for example, there are 14,000 genotypes described (Zeven and Zeven, 1976). In the case of maize, 32 races have been described only in Mexico until 1952 (Wellhausen *et al.*, 1952). The evolution of nature has generated immense variability which man can and should use for his well being.

2.2 Centres of origin of variability

The evolution and species formation have not happened simultaneously on the whole surface of the earth. Vavilov (1935) mentioned that "distribution of species in the world is not uniform" and gives as example the fact that in Costa Rica and Guatemala, even though they are much smaller in their surface area, one can observe the same number of species as in the whole of North America (excluding Mexico). Based on over 300,000 samples collected in the whole world by Vavilov and his collaborators, he proposed the existence of "8 centres of origin of agriculture or, to be precise, 8 independent region where some plants, different for each region, were cultivated for the first time".

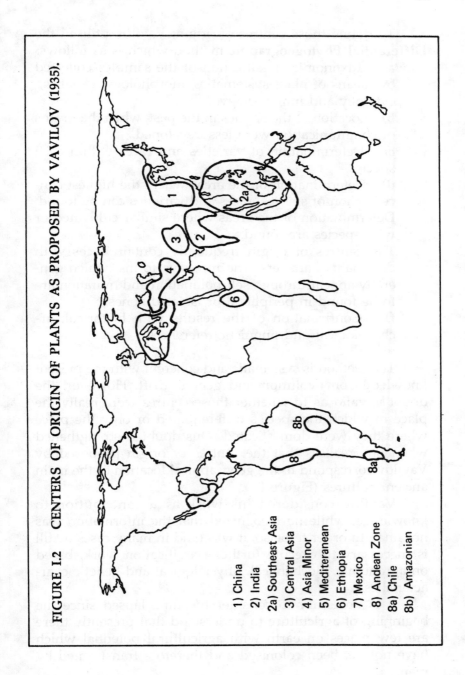

FIGURE I.2   CENTERS OF ORIGIN OF PLANTS AS PROPOSED BY VAVILOV (1935).

1) China
2) India
2a) Southeast Asia
3) Central Asia
4) Asia Minor
5) Mediteranean
6) Ethiopia
7) Mexico
8) Andean Zone
8a) Chile
8b) Amazonian

To define those centres of origin, Vavilov utilised the **Differential Phytogeographic** method which is as follows:

a) Taxonomic classification of the samples collected by means of plant systematics, morphology, genetics, cytology and immunology.

b) Location of the species in the past, when the means of communication were less developed.

c) Determination of varieties and races within each species.

d) Determination of the areas where the highest concentration of species, races and varieties can be found. Determination of the areas where similar cultivated or wild species are found.

The centres of origin frequently contain races with dominant characters. The recessive forms, which generally appear through self-pollination and mutation are to be found in peripheral or isolated zones.

f) Confirmation of the results with historical, archaeological and linguistic references.

The method is systematic and coherent with the present knowledge on evolution and genetic drift. However, the doubt is valid as to whether those centres were really the place in which the species differentiated or only the place where they were domesticated. This doubt is strengthened when one realises that the centres of origin proposed by Vavilov correspond to the geographical location of the main ancient cultures (Figure I.2).

Vavilov considered his work as a contribution to knowledge, while he recognized that the information was not final. In order to be so, it was (and in many cases it still is) necessary to execute further classification work, based on agronomic, biochemical, physiological and genetic characteristics.

It is necessary to consider the time lapsed since the beginning of agriculture to understand that presently there are few places on earth with agricultural potential which have not yet been colonised and therefore transformed by man.

Plant species have a great movement capacity, even more so than the capacity of animals, due to their dissemination via seeds. Gilberth (1895) presents a list of species transported by 5 agents (gravity, water, air, animals and mechanical expulsion) with 10 different natural methods and 55 modifications. It is necessary to add commerce and colonising traits of man and the consequent movements of plants over the last 3,000 years.

Therefore, it is not reasonable to suppose that the distribution of plants which we observe at present is the one which existed at the moment of origin of the species millions of years ago, not even the distribution 200 years ago. There are species which presently are in the process of formation, whose centre of origin we know, as in the extreme case of triticale. This plant was created in Canada a decade ago. In other cases, the doubt has increased over the last few years as to the real centres of origin of species and their cultivated forms. Today it seems adequate to accept the proposition by Harlan (1951, 1975) to classify the origin of plants into centres and non-centres of variability.

2.3 Centres and Non-centres of Variability

The terms used in modern science are changing and in certain cases it is necessary to create new terms in order to define attributes which can hardly be described with socially or formally accepted words. The terms proposed by Harlan (1971) to differentiate the types of distribution of certain species is "non-centres".

Enlarging the definition of Vavilov, Harlan proposes the following groups of species classified according to their distribution:

a) Endemical: Centre of origin of the species can be defined; absence of plants of this species in other areas.

b) Semi-endemical: Centre of origin can be defined due to a very limited distribution of this species.

c) Monocentrical: Centre of origin can be defined and is unique; absence of secondary centres of diversifica-

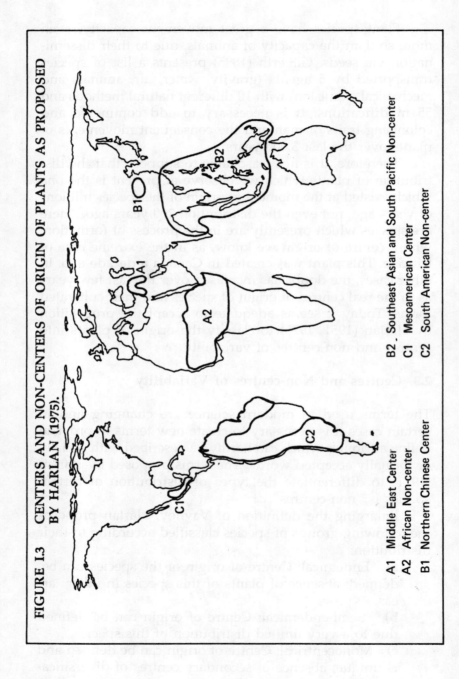

FIGURE 1.3   CENTERS AND NON-CENTERS OF ORIGIN OF PLANTS AS PROPOSED
              BY HARLAN (1975).

A1 Middle East Center   B2 Southeast Asian and South Pacific Non-center
A2 African Non-center   C1 Mesoamerican Center
B1 Northern Chinese Center   C2 South American Non-center

tion.

d) Oligocentric: Centre of origin can be defined with a wide distribution; one or various secondary centres of diversification.

e) Non-centrical: Centres of origin and diversification in different places; it is possible that the plants were domesticated simultaneously in many places.

Based on this classification, Harlan (1975) defines the centres and non-centres of variability for certain cultivated species (Figure I.3). In Appendix I, the definition of centre of origin of variability as defined by Vavilov (1935) is joined with the information by Harlan (1975) and other authors, for some cultivated plants of present or potential importance for the tropics.

If we try to trace the site of origin of any species, it would not be possible to do so because most species originated millions of years ago and have since then multiplied and dispersed over large areas. Efforts are made to clarify if today we can find at least the general areas of origin. The question is of historical interest, as it allows us to know who should be thanked for having contributed a certain plant for the welfare of mankind.

On the other hand, a pragmatic vision of the plant breeder makes him look more for the place where variability can be found now. The existence of microcentres of variability (small areas with a very large variability for a certain species), is one of the results and can be obtained starting with the previous definitions. In each one of the five types of species, it is possible to find areas in which a potential variability which has not been utilised can still be found.

3. USE OF PLANTS BY HUMANITY

Animals eat plants which surround them in a selective way. It is quite rare to find a cow intoxicated by eating one of the many poisonous plants which surround it. The capacity to differentiate between these dangerous plants and nourishing plants already exist in animals less developed than man. Before the consolidation of agriculture, the hunter-gatherer used a wide range of species for food and medicine. While gathering plants, he increased his knowledge as to the plants he could eat without being harmed, discovering those which were toxic and those which cured him. This information was transmitted from generation to generation until the information became so abundant that, in the case of medicinal plants, knowledge had to be accumulated in a specialised person: the medicine man or sorcerer.

Harlan (1975) describes that nowadays the aborigines in Australia, one of the few groups of hunters-gatherers who still survive, use between 74 and 250 different plants. If one adds up the food value of these plants in a typical gatherer's diet, this diet is more balanced in protein and carbohydrates than the diet of most of the modern population in industrialised countries.

The origin of agriculture was a gradual transition, starting with the planting of a few seeds of the most useful plants in the areas surrounding the gatherers' camp, around the stable population centre. It is not probable that this development was due to scarcity of food, as many of the species used by the gatherers were growing in dense natural populations and it was easier to harvest without having to plant.

Lee and Devore (1968; cited by Harlan, 1975) say: "Man has been on earth for approximately 2,000,000 years. During 99% of this time he has lived as a hunter-gatherer. Only 10,000 years ago he started domesticating plants and animals and is living fewer than 200 years in an industrial society. Until today, life as a hunter-gatherer has been the most successful and persistent adaptation to the environment that the human being has achieved". It is necessary to add though that until 10,000 years ago there were never more than 10 million inhabitants to feed on earth and now we are at 5 billion.

3.1 Beginning of agriculture and its consequences

Agriculture is the participation of man in one or many phases of the plant cycle, in addition to the harvest, in order to obtain from it some kind of benefit. As agriculture establishes, we also see the beginning of the struggle of man against certain plants, the specialisation and selection of plants, even though at the beginning it was within the frame work of respect for his environment.

It is no longer a matter of collecting a little bit of each thing, but it becomes necessary that there be a certain order in the cultivated areas, as the various species planted (monoculture comes much later) are useful by definition. New species appear in the fields and whether these are useful or not depends on the species and on the knowledge of the peasant.

A maize field in the central valleys of Oaxaca, Mexico (Azurdia, 1980) had 214 "weeds" which were not eliminated by the producer, as he had a specific use for each one. He would therefore never fumigate with pesticides. The same field in the United States would be considered a disaster by the North American farmer, who has a different approach to agriculture, according to the power of pesticides given him to be used for higher yields of the one crop he plants and knows; even if it poisons the earth for future generations. The peasant has a more unified view of life and a higher culture, even though in the short run he will not obtain the same yield in maize as the North American farmer.

Table I.2 presents a list of the 50 most important cultivated species in the world. A quick look allows us to see how small the number of really important species is. If we compare this information with the 250 species collected by the Australian Aborigines or with the 214 species of "weeds" in the fields of Oaxaca just described, we can see that modern man depends on a much smaller variability, and is therefore much more susceptible to changes in both the environment and to economic changes.

In the world list of species, we can see that the crops belong to the following families:

Table I.2 The 50 main crops in the world, by surface planted in 1986. Taken from FAO (1987).

Crop	Botanical Family	Planted area (1000 of hectares)	Production (thousand tonnes)					
			World	Range	Third World	Range	Industrialized Countries	Range
Wheat	Gramineae	235226	443401	2	157627	4	285826	1
Unhulled rice	Gramineae	143767	396222	43	70927	2	25411	11
Maize	Gramineae	126059	421667	3	148214	5	273288	2
Barley	Gramineae	81125	156977	7	21367	14	135670	5
Soyabean	Leguminosae	50523	86041	10	29026	10	56885	7
Sorghum	Gramineae	44044	64392	12	42866	9	21526	14
Millets	Gramineae	40090	27742	17	259374	3	1832	31
Cotton	Malvaceae	34468	43119	14	24352	11	18782	15
Oats	Gramineae	25691	42596	15	2045	36	40563	9
Dry beans	Leguminosae	24287	13455	24	11201	21	2255	27
Potatos	Solanaceae	21014	291086	5	82369	8	208988	4
Peanuts (Unhulled)	Leguminosae	18535	18535	22	16521	16	2006	30
Rye	Gramineae	15078	24984	19	1979	37	22995	12
Sugarcane	Gramineae	13578	761264	1	693551	16	7796	6
Cassava	Euforbiaceae	13507	123630	8	123630	6	0	0
Sunflower seeds	Compositae	12273	14396	23	3317	33	11048	16
Rapeseeds	Brassicaceae	11488	11132	25	5286	23	5913	21
Green coffee	Rubiaceae	10169	5257	36	5257	24	1	47
Grapes	Vitaceae	9851	66169	11	13579	18	52604	8
Chickpeas	Leguminosae	9530	5947	32	5846	22	101	42

Crop	Family							
Sweet potato	Convolvulaceae	3766						
Dry peas	Leguminosae	7450	8508	28	3171	34	5359	22
Sesame	Pedaliaceae	6479	1963	42	1961	38	3	46
Hemp	Linaceae	5448	2452	41	1293	42	1161	34
Cocoa in grain	Esterculiaceae	4728	1693	44	1693	40	0	0
Tobacco (raw)	Solanaceae	4028	5563	34	3444	32	2119	29
Dry Faba beans	Leguminosae	3689	4283	38	3798	29	488	35
Jute and oth. fibres	Malvaceae	2715	3684	39	3634	31	49	45
Tomatos	Solanaceae	2399	51430	13	20304	15	31124	10
Yam	Dioscoreaceae	2391	23676	20	23532	12	143	41
The	Theaceae	2326	1856	43	1620	41	235	38
Lentils	Leguminosae	1998	1191	45	1001	44	189	39
Watermellon	Cucurbitaceae	1785	25320	18	16301	17	9079	18
Cabbage	Brassicaceae	1631	34421	16	12680	19	21738	13
Dry onions	Liliaceae	1597	21100	1	11871	20	9231	17
Castor seed plant	Euforbiaceae	1451	839	47	785	47	55	44
Linen Fibre	Linaceae	1395	628	48	163	49	462	36
Safflower seeds	Compositae	1383	958	46	801	46	162	40
Taro	Araceae	1047	5585	33	5153	25	436	37
Chillies and peppers	Solanaceae	968	7081	29	4349	27	2730	24
Cucumber	Cucurbitaceae	829	10961	26	4790	26	6171	20
Green peas	Leguminosae	770	4627	37	823	45	3806	23
Sisal	Amarilidaceae	711	506	49	501	48	0	0
Cauliflower	Brassicaceae	543	7058	30	1823	39	2638	26
Melons	Cucurbitaceae	539	6956	31	4277	28	2680	25
Squashes	Cucurbitaceae	527	5360	35	3693	30	1666	32
Carrots	Umbeliferae	504	10465	27	2842	35	7621	19
Hemp fibre	Urticaceae	487	237	50	153	50	864	3
Green beans	Leguminosae	429	2698	40	1187	43	1511	33

NOTE: The range is the position by importance for the 50 crops in the world as a whole and for the 2 groups of countries.

Family	Number of species
Gramineae	9
Leguminosae	9
Solanaceae	4
Cucurbitaceae	4
Others (18 families)	24
TOTAL	50

Therefore, more than half of the main cultivated species in the world correspond to only four families.

3.2 Tendencies in the development of modern agriculture

At present, all "underdeveloped" countries try to increase their agricultural productivity. To achieve that, they have taken a series of guidelines from technologically more advanced countries. In general, the transitional steps from traditional to modern agriculture are: mechanisation of agriculture to reduce labour costs; increase use of inputs to obtain higher yields; use of chemical control of weeds, pathogens and insects; and use of modern-bred varieties.

The technological package, in order to be efficient, needs all the elements to be introduced simultaneously, due to the inter-independence among each other.

In Figure I.4 we can see the flow of genetic material in a traditional agricultural system. The traditional techniques of seed selection maintain the variability of the plant population, in which there is tolerance to local pests. The presence of "weeds" is not considered a problem as the weed population density is kept low through cultural practices or the "weeds" have some known use. The interaction of the crop with the environment is such, that it allows the introduction and preservation of genetic characteristics which exist outside of the cultivated field. As the notion of weed is not so clearly marked as in the modern agricultural system, varieties of species which are not part of the crop

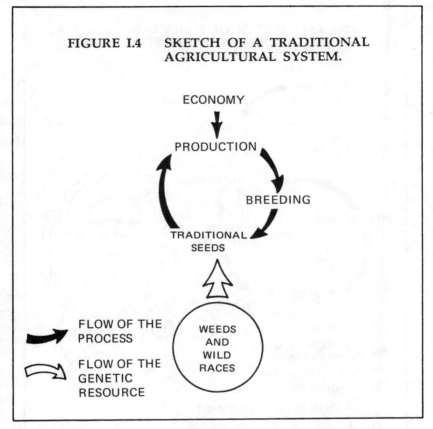

FIGURE I.4   SKETCH OF A TRADITIONAL AGRICULTURAL SYSTEM.

but which could serve as genetic resources to other crops are also preserved.

In Figure I.5 one can see what happens in a high-technology agricultural system. The economy is no longer an external factor, but it has a direct influence on the mode of production. The proposal to mechanise agriculture leads to the need for uniform crops. In order to have uniform crops, it is necessary to have a breeding programme which conducts crossing and selection to generate genetically homogeneous varieties.

For modern breeding, three types of genetic materials are used: modern-bred varieties, traditional varieties and wild forms. Modern varieties, which are widely planted, generally displace traditional seeds. These modern varieties

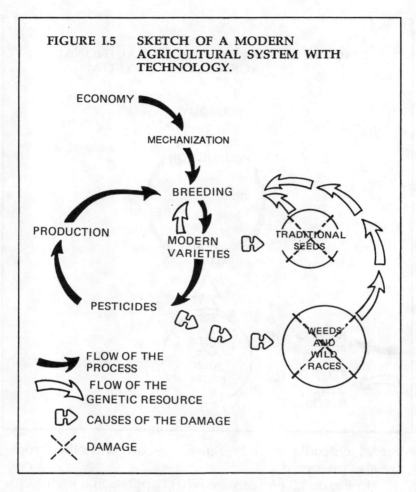

FIGURE I.5   SKETCH OF A MODERN
             AGRICULTURAL SYSTEM WITH
             TECHNOLOGY.

are more susceptible to new forms of pests and diseases
than the traditional ones, and it becomes necessary to fumigate against pests, which themselves adapt to the changes,
and against "weeds" and wild forms, which are then reduced in their numbers.

A few years after the beginning of this process, the
modern variety, because it is uniform not only morpho-
logically but also in its resistance to pests and its capacity
to adapt to changes in the environment, must be replaced
by a new variety which is resistant to the newly evolved
pests.

When this cycle has repeated itself a few times, the only material available for breeding are the modern-bred varieties. This process has already happened in a series of European countries, where presently the breeding programmes and agriculture in general are under serious threat. In the near future, this would be the most evident technical consequence of the model of technological development which is presently being applied on genetic resources.

A classical example of this is the case of wheat. In 1916, leaf-rust destroyed 2 million bushels of wheat in the United States and 1 million bushels in Canada. Similar diseases damaged the wheat producing areas in those countries in 1935 and 1953. At present, wheat varieties in almost all of the United States have to be replaced every five years, after which they are susceptible to the pests which have evolved (NAS, 1972).

However, there are two ways out of this trap: either we change the way western countries propose agricultural production; or we preserve the genetic resources which are the wild species and the traditional varieties which are disappearing. The peasants and some breeders do it for their own interest and, since the last few decades, it is being done at institutional, governmental and transnational levels in gene banks.

Another one of the characteristics of modern agriculture is specialisation. Areas which for a long time produced different crops with a considerable genetic variability, are presently specialising in one or two crops only. An example of that is the reduction of diversified mixed cropping and the introduction of monoculture in tropical countries. Some fruit trees which were planted in those areas may have had a great potential for exploitation and utilisation, but we will never know as they have disappeared.

Nicaraguan women planting Ipecac (*Cephaelis ipecacuanha*), a medicinal plant that has not been studied enough to know the adequate planting methods, to avoid these working conditions.

II
Types of genetic resources and their importance

MAN HAS GROUPED PLANTS into species in an arbitrary way, in order to find some kind of logic in the functioning of nature. When one talks of the kinds of genetic resources, these can be classified into major groups based on different parameters.

A typical economic botanist's classification is based on general use (medicinal, food source, etc.) and specific use (anti-diarrhea, source of carbohydrates, etc.). The classification by industrialised countries in the area of genetic resources is based on the colonial view of the technology applied on the sample under study. If the sample has been obtained from a peasant in the Third World, it will be a "primitive variety", independent of whether it is a plant in the process of domestication or a variety used and enhanced over two thousand years.

These classifications are not satisfactory for the work in places which have a dynamic use of genetic resources that have not yet been stabilised. The proposal is made in this book to classify plants into two big groups, "conventional species" and "non-conventional" species.

On the one side, those plants which are widely used at national and international levels, known for their botanical and agronomic characteristics, and with which the modern scientific breeder knows what he should do in order to obtain better quality and quantity. These plants are "conventional", as there are methods and rules for their breeding and production in modern agriculture. They correspond essentially to the species with the highest production volume in the world.

For those plants, there are breeding programmes which need specific characteristics for their breeding, be it from plants of the species in question, or of similar wild species. Therefore, the concept of "conventional species" includes also those other species whose main function is to breed the main species, as for example the wild potatoes species used to get better disease resistance in the cultivated potatoes *Solanum tuberosum.*

On the other hand, there is a great number of "nonconventional" species, about which little or nothing at all is known in the areas of genetics and agronomy. The only one who knows something about these plants is the peasant when it is already locally cultivated, the medicine man if it is a medicinal plant which is gathered, or nobody if it is a plant which is still growing in the wild, yet to be domesticated.

1.   CONVENTIONAL SPECIES

Conventional species are used in breeding programmes, considered genetic resources at the international level and used by modern science.

In the case of the genetic resources used in breeding programmes, it is important to know if they are in danger of extinction or not, according to the intensity of a series of factors. Traditional maize in Mexico is used in breeding programmes. At the same time, modern-bred varieties are recommended and sometimes imposed on peasants by the means of credit, i.e. credit is given only to those peasants who   plant modern-bred varieties of maize. This brings about the elimination of fields with traditional maize and the breeder has to go back to the germplasm banks to get useful genes. Eventhough at present there are wide collections of maize in Mexico, some areas have been barely worked on, especially tropical maize in the Yucatan and Chiapas states.

A specific example could be the maize of Jala, known for its big size (ears of up to 60 cm. in length), which during the author's collecting trip to the area of Jala, Nayarit, in June 1982, it had apparently disappeared. According to the peasants, Jala maize could not "compete" with the hybrid, as it was getting contaminated with pollen from the hybrid which was widely planted in the area. Fortunately, there is maize of this kind in the germplasm bank of the Ministry of Agriculture in Mexico.

1.1 Breeding for the quality of the product

When Man cultivates plants, he always does it for profits. This profit will be determined by the quality of the produce he obtains from the plants, which can be either directly utilised for food or transformed for further use.

The quality will be determined by the objective of the crop. In the case of plants cultivated as a source of food, the goal of quality refers to the contents of protein, carbohydrates, fats, vitamins and minor elements. On top of that, it is important that products should be adapted to the expectations of the people who will be purchasing and consuming them, as this will determine if the produce is finally consumed or not. The main factor in formal quality is taste. If the product is not pleasant to be eaten, or is not accepted due to prevailing eating habits, even if the product is very good from a biochemical point of view, it will not be eaten. In industrialised society, the problem is even more complex, as propaganda has made the shape, colour and size of the product more important for the consumer than the food value or the taste.

The last determining element for the quality of food species is its storage and processing potential. A large part of the harvest of food plants nowadays are processed before they are consumed. It is therefore very important to make a variety that can be easily transformed industrially or even at home. In Central America certain types of beans with very good taste characteristics, are not accepted by the population because it takes too long to cook them, with the consequence of greater   use of fuel in the cooking process.

In the case of oil sources, a better quality implies that the oil originating from this plant has the needed balance

of saturated and unsaturated fats, the existence of particular substances, that it is easy to extract, and that the fibre
content is low. In the case of rapeseed (*Brassica napus*), low
erucic acid contents varieties have been selected for human
consumption and others with high erucic acid contents, to
be used for lubricants production (CIGI, 1982).

In fibre crops, the fibre length, resistance and ease of
processing are determining factors and there are excellent
sources of variability; for instance, the cotton Acala was
collected in Mexico during the winter of 1906 close to the
village of Acala, Oaxaca. Currently, this cotton, after a selection programme, is the main cotton planted in California. It is also cultivated in Rio Grande in Texas and in
New Mexico. The Egyptian cotton was introduced in 1903
from the Nile area and then, after some selections, is now
one of the most widely planted types in North America
(Poehlman, 1965).

Medicinal plants or alkaloid sources are considered to
be better when a large proportion of the obtained molecules
belong to the active alkaloid group as (opposed) to the in-
active alkaloids. In Nicaragua, selection is being made on
plants of ipecac (*Cephaelis ipecacuanha*) to obtain a higher
content of emetine and a reduction of cefeline. Medicinal
plants are also better when the concentration of active sub-
stance is increased, in order to get higher yields and for
easier extraction. A typical case is the breeding in India of
opium poppy (*Papaver somniferum*) to increase the concentrations of alkaloids for the production of morphine.

1.2 Increase in yields

When a variety has good quality characteristics, it is important to increase the quantity produced. Other varieties
may be of inferior quality but have higher yields. Efforts
are made to use the good characteristics of both varieties to
obtain a new one with high yields and good product quality.
It is not very frequent that a variety with high yield is a
wild species. By using traditional varieties and modern
varieties over the last 40 years, it has been possible to in-

crease significantly the yield of many crops.

1.3 Tolerance to adverse factors

Considering all the adverse factors which can harm a plant (environment, pests and pathogens), the idea arises quite naturally that wild species will be more resistant. In general, a species in the wild has to survive in a more adverse environment than the cultivated ones, which are protected by man. Breeding programmes of wheat would be in serious trouble if "primitive" varieties did not exist which are resistant to certain races of rust to which the modern varieties are susceptible. Breeding programmes in Canada, the United States and Europe have made systematic use of this variability.

In the case of tropical pastures, one of the major problems is aluminium toxicity. For that reason, the International Centre for Tropical Agriculture (CIAT) has systematically collected wild ecotypes of pasture plants in Central America in order to select all those which tolerate acidic soil. This is one case in which a breeding programme with hybridising is not necessary, but one can directly evaluate the selected wild resource.

2. NON-CONVENTIONAL SPECIES

As was mentioned before, non-conventional species are those which have not entered the "official" chain of breeding, production and marketing. In this category one would have many of the native species from the tropics, which until now have been locally used without the formal support of modern research and development programmes.

The potential of these genetic resources has been rarely evaluated, even though in the industrialised countries they are considered more important every day. For example, in the case of *Amaranthaceae* (Amaranth) and *Quenopodiaceae*, there are research centres in the United States which for a long time have been studying the potential use of these crops on a larger scale (Bailey, 1977). A series of books by the

United States National Academy of Sciences (NAS, 1975, 1977, 1979) presents the potential of under-exploited crops and non-conventional species. Beyond the known potential, it is important to avoid their disappearance. Esquinas (1983) mentions that these are the species which will most probably disappear. Even if they were not to disappear as species, the cultivated forms, often the results of hundreds or thousands of years of selection, would be lost.

Presently in Mexico, there are at least 40 species under those circumstances, from fruit trees in Yucatan to the "wheat" of the sea which grows in the waters of the Gulf of Baja California, which are used by only 20 Seri Indian families in Nayarit. They will disappear as cultivated plants because modern agriculture needs uniform production and opens the "agriculture frontier" with conventional species. Peasants have a higher probability of obtaining support if they grow "conventional species" as these are studied by the agricultural research institutions and supported by the credit institutions. Furthermore, they have means to market their harvest easily, without having to establish new marketing channels of their own.

2.1 Non-conventional food resources

One can differentiate food resources between those which are cultivated and those which grow in the wild. The cultivated food resources are not as abundant as the wild ones. In Mexico, the number of cultivated non-conventional species is fewer than 30 (Table II.1). In the category of wild growing food sources, it is almost impossible to determine the number of species used by man. At present, at least 3 research centres in Mexico (The National Institute on Biological Resources, the Institute of Biology of the University of Mexico and the National Institute of Nutrition) are trying to formulate this list. In Mexico alone it is possible to make a modest estimate of 800 wild species which are used for food.

Table II.1 Non-conventional food plants in Mexico

Common Name	Scientific Name
Amaranth	*Amaranthus spp.*
Skin Tomato	*Physalis spp.*
*Huauzontle	*Chenopodium spp.*
*Chirimoya, Guanábana, Anona	*Anona spp.*
Avocado	*Persea spp.*
Pumpkin, Gourd	*Cucurbita spp.*
Lima Bean (Yucátan)	*Phaseolus lunatus*
Scarlet Runner bean (Highland)	*Phaseolus coccineous*
Vanilla	*Vanilla planifolia*
*Chayote	*Sechium edule*
Tania/cocoyam/taro	*Xanthosoma spp.*
*Zapotes (Negro,Blanco)	*Sapotaceae*
Chili	*Capsicum spp.*
*Chilacayote	*Cucurbita ficifolia*
Cashew fruit	*Anacardium occidentale*

* No translation available

2.2 Non-conventional medicinal plants

In this category are all those plants, generally growing wild, which are collected by man to heal. The word "healing" is used in a wide sense, and it includes the healing of non-physiological diseases. According to Erick Estrada (Personal Communication) from the Medicinal Plants Section of the University of Chapingo in Mexico, there are presently 3,000 medicinal plants which have been identified. Every year Estrada has been reporting 50 new species. Of these 3,000 species, 800 have been documented and fewer than 50 have been studied in the laboratory and tested experimentally. Even though it is not probable that these species will disappear immediately, especially as they are not cultivated and have a wide distribution under wild conditions, it is important to collect the most promising ones systematically, because information and knowledge of medicinal plants may disappear even though the resource itself may survive. The number of medicine men up to now has remained constant, but in many cases, they know less than the medicine men of the past. One day, there will be plants which we will know were utilised in the past but we won't know what they were used for.

2.3 Sources of raw materials

In this category are all the species of industrial importance. The potential of forests in tropical countries has been irrationally exploited, as work has centred on very few species. The indiscriminate extraction of cedar (*Cedrella odorata*), mahogany (*Swietenia macrophylla*) and two or three other species of precious timber, has caused a drastic reduction of these in their natural habitat. In these cases, unless irrational extraction stops, it is absolutely necessary to collect the genetic resources in order to maintain variability. Otherwise, in the near future there will be no means to reforest with these species. On top of that, a series of wood species have not been studied which could serve a more efficient and diversified timber industry. There are also species which are used locally as sources of fibres, resins and gums which have to be studied in more depth. In the museum of the Forest Institute in Dehra Dun, India, there is an exhibit of resins obtained from wood species, out of which only two are used, even then only on a medium scale.

3. Wild species and species of use in the past

This group of species is the largest and the one which needs most research. In many cases of species which have not yet been used, it is possible that there may be a potential for utilization which has not been studied or which has been forgotten. It is urgent to listen and register the knowledge of those who know the use of the plants but many are losing the collective memory in our countries with traditions which have survived for millenia due to the rapid changes wrought by industrialization.

Large tracts of tropical forests have not been described yet. These forests are potential sources of alkaloids, raw materials and food. Only gradually are researchers working on them. In the Amazon jungle, Schultes (1982) studied the sources of alkaloids for use by the United States Army, learning the possible uses of the plants from the indigenous people. In the Lacandone jungle in Mexico, alternatives have been studied for the timber industry. In the arid zones of Mexico, jojoba (*Simondsia chinensis*) is being studied as well as guayule (*Parthenium argentatum*). Soya bean was an almost unknown crop to the Western world, and after 40 years it is now the ninth most important crop in the world.

Reviewing the writings of the chroniclers, many useful species are described there which were used in the past. Fernandez de Oviedo in 1562 described more than 50 species which were used in Mexico at the time of the Spanish invasion. Some of them are not used anymore. In other cases, only one is being used when the description by a chronicler enables us to postulate the existence of various species which were used.

Mexican peasant in Puebla, harvesting his traditional crop of maize. This plant has evolved since the domestication of primitive teozintle through the work of this man and his ancestors.

III
Genetic Resources: Dilemma

THE FIRST QUESTION which one can ask is whether genetic resources should be preserved or utilised. If one is talking of preservation of resources in the Third World, it must be with the clarity that the final objective is the utilisation of those resources in a few years' time. The main reason why genetic resources should be preserved can be summarised in three aspects:

1.   Genetic resources are, as a matter of fact, crops presently cultivated by peasants in many parts of the world. Due to the advances in modern agricultural technology and the expansion of agriculture into previously uncultivated lands, which is happening out of the control of the peasant (who very often does not own the land), a larger part of this material is in danger of disappearing very quickly. In Europe and other industrialised countries they have already disappeared, which validates this argument even more for the Third World.

2.   The various collection of species made in the past have not been adequately preserved. The problem happens in all countries and takes place even in international institutions like the International Centre for Maize and Wheat Breeding (CIMMYT), with abundant budget and scientists dedicated full time to preserve the resources (Timothy and Goodman, 1979).

3.   Plant breeding programmes have generally very limited scope and objectives and the genetic base of the material used is generally narrow and common to all varieties. As a consequence, there is a risk of intensive damage

to the crops by pests and diseases. It is necessary to introduce a larger genetic variability in the cultivated varieties in order to protect them in the event of epidemic diseases.

This problem is marked in the industrialised countries. In 1970, an epidemic caused by the rust *Helminthosporium maydis* in the United States reduced the production of maize in the attacked fields down to 50% and the total production of the country by 15%, which caused losses of hundreds of millions of dollars. The special commission convened to analyse the causes (NAS, 1972) concluded that the cause was genetic uniformity, as most of the maize hybrids in that country had been developed using only one source of parental sterility (Texas cytoplasm, for cytoplasmic sterility) which was susceptible to the new rust races which have developed. The study recommended mainly genetic diversification and the constant search for new genetic resources to avoid the problem from happening again. There are at least four reported cases of similar magnitude in history.

As can be seen, the worries about genetic resources and variability have strong effects on the development of agriculture, and therefore on the development of food production for the future of mankind. A worry which started in the 1950s and was initially little shared, became a stronger movement supported by scientists in all countries. When it became clear that genetic resources had an economic importance, a discussion started about the rights over them. This is basically an economic and political discussion, as it is not solved on the basis of rights or logic but rather the power of those in the discussion. To solve the technical and economic problems which have been presented, national and international organisations were created which are described in the second part of this chapter.

1.   WHOM DO THE GENETIC RESOURCES BELONG TO?

Over the last 15 years, industrialised countries hear voices claiming rights over certain plants. As strange as it may sound these voices do not come from developing countries, out of which almost all plants of economic importance for the "First World" have come at no cost but it was a claim from the breeders, and scientists who demanded payment for their author's rights over the plants they had bred (UPOV, 1981). The idea of plant breeders'rights have always been going around in the breeders circles but never had significant repercussions. It is only in the last few years, when practically no independent breeders subsisted and when the production of commercial varieties was in the hands of great national and transnational corporations, that laws on plant patenting have been approved and enlarged in the industrialised countries. This is due to the interest of transnational corporations to "protect their investments" as they say, to make sure people can never get again what they initially gave for free.

Breeding programmes use three types of genetic resources: wild materials, traditional varieties, frequently and wrongly called "primitive" (wrongly, because "primitive" is whatever has its origin in a previous absence, not in thousands of years' work as our native traditional varieties), and finally, "modern-bred" varieties, including breeders' lines.

As every one of these types is part of breeding programmes, there should be free and unrestricted exchange of all three types of genetic resources or no exchange at all (Querol, 1983).

The reality is that free exchange is frequently a myth. Various countries have restricted the free exchange: the United States embargoed, for political reasons, the genetic resources which Nicaragua needed, including seeds which had been collected in Nicaragua itself. Something similar also happened to Afghanistan, Albania, Cuba, Iran and Libya (Mooney, 1983).

Melaku Worede (Personal communication), Director of the Plant Genetic Resources Centre in Ethiopia, country of origin of a series of crops of world economic importance, mentions that the country, tired of giving away its resources for the enrichment of the industrialised countries, has closed its borders to the resources indiscriminate exit. Trevor

Williams (Personal Communication), states that for industrial crops, Brazil and India have had similar attitudes.

If one takes as an example *Cacahuazintle* maize, a traditional Mexican variety, of large size and excellent yields, and considered a genetic resource for free exchange, why shouldn't one regard modern bred maize or the lines for the production of hybrids of a transnational seeds corporation as a genetic resource for free exchange?

1.1 Whom do the plants belong to?

Without getting into all legal aspects of property and their social implications, as a matter of definition, everything which is to be found within a certain space is considered to belong to the humans who occupy it (due to our anthropocentric view). History, culture, earth, water, minerals, the sources of energy and the plants and animals are of the person, the people, the nation or humanity, depending on the physical limits which one establishes.

The humanistic vision of the European philosophers of the 18th century defined knowledge and notions such as beauty and justice as universal, and therefore, the patrimony of humanity.

Private property, which implies in its definition the value that an object has for someone, was enlarged and consolidated by the industrial society by including ideas into the private property domain, so that new solutions could be patented. Thus, not only are objects subject to property, but even ideas. The patenting of ideas, which was regulated in the Paris Convention of 1883, was then philosophically based on the notion of "human rights" of the person who invented, forgetting the rights of society which forms and maintains the inventor and which gives him the basis of information and knowledge for him to develop his ideas.

Starting with the previous proposition, it is evident that plants have owners. In the case of plants which have been bred for thousands of years by the human population of a certain region, it is the offspring (in the widest sense) of the old inhabitants, who have the right to demand a payment for the object: the plants transformed through man's work. In the case of wild species, nations, through their states, have the right to value their raw materials or even their ornamental plants.

The movement of genetic resources has always been from colonies and "under-developed" countries towards their imperial centres. The value of plants has been known for thousands of years; they are the foundation of all development, and they have been one of the objectives of many of the large conquest wars until the 19th century. However, through a conceptual jump which is difficult to accept, these plants have been defined as the "patrimony of humanity". Based on that, Europe and presently all industrialised countries, were supplied with resources which they needed and still need, without cost or compensation, for the 'well-being of humanity'.

1.2 Whom do the varieties belong to?

Plants are grouped according to parameters used by the person who classifies. The parameters used by Linnaeus in order to classify plants were based on characteristics of flowers and fruits. These are still being used for the definition of botanical species. After the classification by species, these are subdivided into varieties according to morphological characteristics and to human interests.

The definition of a "variety" has been a major difficulty due to the variability which exists in nature. This in principle excludes the possibility to delimit a group of plants, unless all of the components are described. This would mean to define each one of the alleles present in the population and the frequency of each one.

There is an artificial differentiation between traditional varieties, bred by peasants during thousands of years of work (which in the Northern countries are called "primitive") and modern varieties (called "cultivars" in the Northern countries) which have been bred by western-styled scientists maybe for 5 to 15 years. The main difference relating to genetic variability is that the former maintain a wide genetic variability and are clearly different among themselves, whereas the latter have a uniform genetic base and are differentiated among them by a relatively low number of alleles. At the country level, the former are in the Third World and the latter mainly in industrialised countries, where strong modern breeding programmes exist.

Traditional as well as modern varieties are the result of work by man on plants. The answer as to who owns the varieties is only partly clear; breeding work has been done by one or many people, be it selecting good seeds for next year's planting, or introducing a new gene for disease resistance by means of biotechnology or modern breeding methods. The second part of the question is still unanswered, which is, who owns the matter which has been worked on.

1.3 Whom do the genes belong to?

If one were to go all the way to the genetic level, one must raise the same question. The alleles and their combinations are to be located in defined geographical spaces. The frequency of the different alleles these plants contain is determined by natural selection and the work by man on those plants. In the case of wild plants, the genes are part of the patrimony of the geographic space in which they are to be found; they belong to the nation. In the case of plants selected by men and women, the presence of certain alleles can be due to the selection which increase their frequency, which merits at least recognition, but not as individual property, as there was no appropriation of the matter worked on since the beginning. Those genes are still the patrimony of the nation. To think that the alleles belong to those who identify them would be the equivalent of saying that radium belongs to the Curie family because they isolated it. It also means that a country which does not have the capital or the technology to use its uranium ore automatically loses sovereignty over those resources.

As a conclusion, it seems that both logic and ethics tell us that genetic resources, in whatever shape, are the patrimony of the nations where they originated. Authority over those resources will increase as nations use those resources themselves. It is therefore necessary to create national genetic resources programmes.

2. NATIONAL GENETIC RESOURCES PROGRAMMES

Plant genetic resources programmes will have specific organisation characteristics peculiar to each country, considering the wide range of possibilities which are available. These range from the simple conservation of the resources by peasants who have always preserved them up till now to the establishment of a proper advanced programme for the collection and systematic use of available genetic resources, which would include biotechnology. These alternatives are not necessarily mutually exclusive, and their interaction will allow for real use of the resources.

Genetic resources should not only be placed in a museum-like national programme, service or agricultural research organisation, but they should also be preserved and utilised by peoples' organisations. Peasant communities, organisations and cooperatives are an excellent means to coordinate and preserve genetic resources, as they have been historically the collectors, curators and breeders of those resources. Genetic variability originated since thousands of years ago through the work of peasants, and is evidently quite well preserved by them. Specific responsibility of conservation, therefore, can be directly supported by those groups.

It is essential that all the available information be really available. The absence of a national coordinating body, in the hands of the nation or its representatives, causes a multiplicity of functions and, as a final result, the inefficient use of available human and economic resources. The support for peasants and farmers communities for the conservation of their resources can be the most efficient means for the preservation of resources, their rational utilisation. It will be possible mainly depending on how much these traditional groups are supported.

2.1 Principles and aims

The principles approved for the national genetic resources programmes in Nicaragua (MIDINRA, 1983) and Peru (INIPA, 1986), with some differences, are:

● Genetic resources have an economic, cultural and political values.
● Genetic resources which exist in a country are the patrimony of the nation. Their appropriation or export is a right of the people of the country. The handing over of genetic material to other countries is an expression of goodwill from the people of that country and will be done only in the framework of full reciprocity.
● The exchange of genetic resources should be controlled by legislation which includes genetic resources, modern varieties and the production, certification and marketing of seeds.
● Genetic resources are associated with knowledge by peasants and other field practitioners who are empirical researchers. The study, collection and utilisation of these make it absolutely necessary that theoretical researchers recover and understand this great reservoir of knowledge.
● The collection and conservation of genetic resources are a means for their rational utilisation, having as a main goal the introduction of these into production.

The aims are to:

● Avoid the loss or underutilisation of genetic material of plants, cattle, and other mammals, birds, fish and of any living organism with present or potential use.
● Support and coordinate the work on and with genetic resources within the country and with other countries for national and international cooperation.
● Propose new crops or variants of crops to be in-

troduced for production.
● Serve as a base for the creation of regional banks of genetic resources.
● Establish the policies for the management and exchange of genetic resources.
● Ensure variability to prevent any threat to the food security of the country.

2.2 Functioning of a genetic resource programme

A genetic resource programme in Latin America, or anywhere in the Third World for that matter, should utilise its own resources as well as external ones. Many species which originated in other areas of the world could be used by those countries, if the similarity in climate permits.

The collection of native germplasm is the most important aspect of such a programme. Unless a priority is established for the crops to be worked on, the volume of material which would have to be collected exceeds the management capacity of any institution. In the case of Peru alone, there are more than a hundred species (INIPA, 1986) which could be collected as under-utilised native species. If from each one of these only 300 samples were taken, a base collection of 30,000 accessions would be reached. There are not enough researchers to characterise, evaluate and specially utilise this huge genetic variability. The first step for the rational use of the human resources available is to establish the priorities in the work of crops to be studied. These priorities must be a function of the needs of the country, generally feeding their population in the first place, and then possibly import-substitution and the development of agro-industry.

Some needs of the population can frequently be solved very quickly with a small increase in the quality or quantity of certain crops. An example of this would be the collection of traditional root and tuber crops or tropical fruit trees in Central America, their evaluation and selection and the immediate redistribution of selected varieties.

The systematic introduction of plants or genetic vari-

FIGURE III.1
CONCEPTUAL FLOW FOR THE UTILISATION OF GENETIC RESOURCES

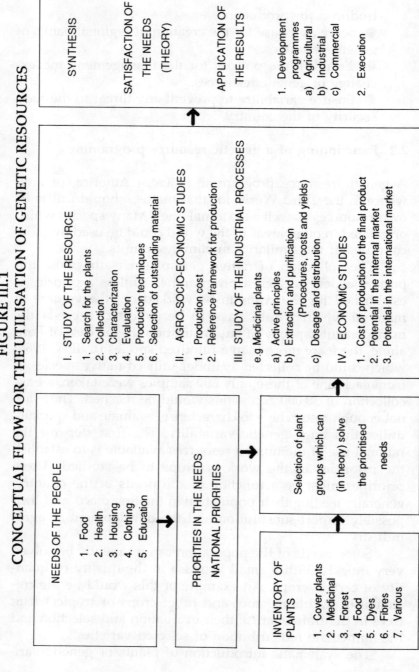

NEEDS OF THE PEOPLE
1. Food
2. Health
3. Housing
4. Clothing
5. Education

PRIORITIES IN THE NEEDS
NATIONAL PRIORITIES

INVENTORY OF PLANTS
1. Cover plants
2. Medicinal
3. Forest
4. Food
5. Dyes
6. Fibres
7. Various

Selection of plant groups which can (in theory) solve the prioritised needs

I. STUDY OF THE RESOURCE
1. Search for the plants
2. Collection
3. Characterization
4. Evaluation
5. Production techniques
6. Selection of outstanding material

II. AGRO-SOCIO-ECONOMIC STUDIES
1. Production cost
2. Reference framework for production

III. STUDY OF THE INDUSTRIAL PROCESSES
e.g Medicinal plants
a) Active principles
b) Extraction and purification (Procedures, costs and yields)
c) Dosage and distribution

IV. ECONOMIC STUDIES
1. Cost of production of the final product
2. Potential in the internal market
3. Potential in the international market

SYNTHESIS

SATISFACTION OF THE NEEDS (THEORY)

APPLICATION OF THE RESULTS
1. Development programmes
   a) Agricultural
   b) Industrial
   c) Commercial
2. Execution

ability is another of the functions of a genetic resources programme which does not limit its activities to the collection of germplasm for long term storage. In Latin America, for example, a series of crops introduced and adapted over the last 500 years, (citrus trees, small grain cereals, fruit trees from South East Asia, and even plants from temperate climate) have limited variability in Latin America itself. The analysis of the situation, the introduction and evaluation of introduced varieties can be a more important contribution to production than breeding of the locally adapted varieties introduced a long time ago.

The concepts developed in the last paragraphs are presented in a simplified scheme in Figure III.1.

2.2.1. Strategy to initiate a programme

A genetic resource programme as an institution has a series of short, medium and long term objectives. Many of the objectives can only be achieved 10 or 20 years after the work is initiated, but they should be clearly stated from the beginning, in order to be executed in the medium term activities.

General objectives
- Collect, introduce, document, preserve and evaluate the genetic resources which could be used in the country.
- Take all those actions which will allow the increase in the number of species utilised in agricultural production and increase the genetic variability within each of the commercial species.
- Support all institutions which are interested in fulfilling the two objectives just mentioned.

Specific Objectives
- Organise a national network of germplasm banks. It is understood that germplasm banks would be cold rooms for the storage of seeds, air-conditioned areas for the storage of plant parts or *in vitro* plants or col-

lection gardens for the storage of adult plants.
● Create an information bank (computerise if possible) of the genetic resources available for the country.
● Link the researchers within and outside of the coordinating institution and establish new research subjects.

Research and infrastructure development goals
● Organise the national germplasm bank for crops which grow from seeds.
● Make an inventory of the other germplasm banks in the country in order to identify missing samples and duplicate them in the national bank.
● Build or adapt cold rooms and air-conditioned areas, for the medium and short term storage of germplasm.
● Study and make an inventory of the genetic variability of the country.
● Establish a regeneration and multiplication programme for the seeds in order to ensure the viability of those stored in the seed banks.
● Install a tissue culture laboratory to develop techniques to free plants from pathogens, for storage and multiplication through tissue culture in the case of major main perennial or vegetatively reproduced plants.
● Establish a network for the management of data and install micro-computers in the participating stations.
● Organise a national herbarium of all useful plants in the country in coordination with existing herbaria.
● Organise the collection gardens in existence and establish adequate zones for other gardens, representative of each species.
● Establish the necessary duplicates to avoid the loss of germplasm.
● Ensure adequate conservation through economic support of people, who have outstanding material, and also support in the form of irrigation systems and physical protection of collection gardens in the existing network.

● Establish, at a medium term, a centre for the study of the quality and potential of native species in the country. Define, characterise and evaluate the maximum possible number of non-conventional species for their better utilisation in the near future.

3. INTERNATIONAL SITUATION

From 1965 until 1973 in the United Nations Food and Agricultural Organisation (FAO), a group of Experts in the Exploration and the Introduction of Plants coordinated the activities within FAO on the subject of collection and introduction of genetic resources. The work was executed by independent groups and consultants who were hired by FAO. In 1973, a series of organisations which depended on FAO studied the problems and in 1974 the Ford and Rockefeller Foundations decided to create the International Board of Plant Genetic Resources (IBPGR) which took over the functions of the board of experts of FAO.

At an international level, there are wide, deep-rooted selfish interests related to the marketing of seeds and genetic resources. Transnational oil corporations have bought up many seeds companies and the economic potential of these is vast if one takes into account the fact that already in 1978 the seeds industry had a retail value of US$10 billion. Mooney (1980) makes an analysis of the implications of this concentration of power on seeds in the hands of a few corporations.

In the following discussion, we will analyse the creation of IBPGR and its role. Later on in the book, the FAO Commission on Plant Genetic Resources will be analysed.

3.1 The International Board of Plant Genetic Resources (IBPGR)

The IBPGR was created by the Ford and Rockefeller Foundations and by some industrialised countries, all of which had created the Consultative Group for International Agriculture Research (CGIAR) a few years ago. The CGIAR had the self-assigned function to guide and serve as avant-garde to agricultural research in Third World countries. This was done through the establishment of international agricultural research centres, but without the control of the United Nations or of the international community, or even of the countries where the centres were to be located.

The network of international centres is distributed in places which are very close to the centre of origin of the crop they work with. These centres have always been very controversial with regard to their legal and political status, even though it cannot be denied that they have had some significant achievements in the Third World, including an increase in yields for the rich farmers in the Third World resulting from an increase in the import of fertilisers and pesticides. To analyse the work on genetic resources of each one of these centres would go beyond the objectives of this book, even though it should be understood that these centres have the biggest genetic resources collections of almost all crops of economic international importance, and store almost a quarter of all the accessions which are in the world (Plucknett *et al.*, 1983).

The IBPGR, since its inception, has had its central offices in the FAO building in Rome, where it has used the infrastructure, the administrative apparatus and even the envelopes with FAO letterhead, but without having to report its administrative work and activities to the national representatives in FAO. Instead, it is accountable to a group of industrialised countries as represented by CGIAR. The objectives of IBPGR, as presented in its report of activities for the 1974-1978 period (IBPGR, 1979) were the following:

1. Identify the general and specific needs for exploration, collection, conservation and evaluation of plant genetic resources, especially in the case of economically important species or its wild and cultivated related varieties. Establish priorities among these species and ensure within the available resources that the preserved material be available for breeding programmes and other scientific activities.

2. Establish points of reference, methods and procedures for the exploration and evaluation of genetic resources. Determine the minimal levels for the conservation and regeneration of seeds and the management of vegetative material.

3. Do whatever is necessary to ensure that duplicates of stored seeds as well as of vegetative material be available.

4. Promote technical meetings and training activities at all levels.

5. Develop a network of institutions, organisations and programmes at the international level which should be capable and willing to contribute to the four above mentioned objectives.

6. Promote the inter-relation of existing programmes in order to avoid unnecessary duplicates and try to complement work in the least studied aspects.

7. Strengthen the programmes of existing organisations and promote the establishment of new organisations, institutions and programmes with the goals just mentioned whenever it is necessary, especially in the areas of greater genetic diversity.

8. Promote the distribution of information and material between the institutional centres and promote, within the limits of available resources, the establishment of an inventory of the collections.

9. Make appropriate recommendations for the management of information from the banks on computers.

Probably in order to be more efficient in its genetic resources collection objectives, the IBPGR presented itself as an organisation directly linked to FAO. In reality, the main IBPGR efforts have been to collect genetic resources in the Third World.

In the annual report in 1986, it is mentioned that "the main mandate of IBPGR is to ensure that genetic resources of cultivated plants be collected and preserved in germplasm banks and that they be therefore accessible for use by plant breeders and other scientists. The main emphasis of IBPGR

Table III.1 Priorities of the IBPGR in 1975 for the collection of genetic resources, by region and crop.

PRIORITIES OF THE REGION	PRIORITY OF THE CROP →	Wheat (1)	Sorghum (1)	Millets (1)	Barley (3)	Rice (2)	Maize (3)	Oats (3)	Rye (3)	Beans (1)	Chickpeas (2)	Peanuts (2)	Soya Beans (2)	Vigna unguiculata, V. sinensis (Caupi) (2)	Vigna spp. asian (2)	Cajanus spp. (3)	Pisum spp. (3)	Vicia faba (3)	Cassava (2)	Potato (2)	Sweet Potato (2)	Dioscorea spp. (Yam) (3)	Bananas (2)	Cotton (2)	Jute (3)	Brassica spp. (3)	Elaeis guineensis (African oilpalm) (3)	Elaeis oleifera (American oilpalm) (2)	Olive (3)	Safflower (3)	Sunflower (3)	Sugar Beet (2)	Sugarcane (2)	Rubber (2)	Coffee (1)	Cocoa (2)
South west Asia	1	×	×	-	1	-	-	×	×	×	×	-	-	-	-	-	×	×	-	-	-	-	-	-	-	×	-	-	×	×	-	1	-	-	×	-
Central Asia	2	×	×	-	1	-	-	×	×	-	×	-	-	-	-	-	×	×	-	×	-	-	-	×	-	×	-	-	×	×	×	×	-	-	-	-
Southeast Asia	2	-	×	×	×	1	×	-	-	×	-	×	×	×	×	×	×	×	×	-	×	×	×	×	×	-	×	×	-	-	×	-	×	×	-	×
Southern Asia	1	-	×	×	×	1	×	-	-	×	×	×	×	×	×	×	×	×	×	-	×	×	×	×	×	×	-	-	-	×	-	-	×	×	-	-
Pacific Islands	3	-	-	-	-	-	-	-	-	×	-	-	-	×	-	-	-	×	×	×	×	×	×	-	-	-	×	-	-	-	-	-	×	-	-	×
Mesoamerica	1	-	-	-	-	-	×	-	-	×	-	×	-	×	-	-	-	×	×	×	×	-	×	×	-	-	-	×	-	-	×	-	-	-	×	-
Andean Zone	2	-	-	-	-	-	×	-	-	×	-	×	-	×	-	×	-	×	×	×	×	-	×	×	-	-	-	×	×	×	×	-	-	-	×	-
Brazil	2	-	-	-	-	-	×	-	-	×	-	×	×	×	-	×	-	×	×	×	×	×	×	×	-	-	-	×	-	×	×	-	×	×	×	-
South of Southamerica	3	-	-	-	×	-	×	×	×	×	×	-	-	-	-	-	×	-	×	×	-	-	-	×	-	-	-	-	×	×	-	×	-	-	-	-
West of Africa	2	-	×	×	-	1	×	-	-	×	-	×	×	×	×	×	×	×	×	-	×	×	×	×	-	-	×	×	×	×	×	-	-	×	×	×
East of Africa	3	-	×	×	-	-	×	-	-	×	-	×	-	×	×	×	×	×	×	-	×	×	×	×	-	-	×	×	×	-	-	-	-	×	×	-
Ethiopia	1	×	×	×	×	-	×	×	×	×	-	×	-	×	×	×	×	×	-	-	-	-	-	×	-	×	-	-	×	×	×	-	-	-	×	-
Orient	3	×	×	-	1	-	×	-	-	×	×	×	×	×	×	×	×	×	×	-	×	×	×	×	×	×	-	-	×	-	×	-	×	×	×	-
Mediterranean	1	×	-	-	1	-	×	×	×	×	×	-	-	×	×	-	×	×	-	-	-	-	×	×	-	×	-	-	×	×	-	1	×	-	×	-

Priorities   1 = Urgent   2 = Very important   3 = Important   x = Priority is determined by the priority of crop is to collect germplasm which has immediate use or is threatened with being eroded. The largest part of what has been collected by IBPGR has been traditional varieties which very often could have contributed in an immediate manner to the breeding of modern varieties. Since the creation of IBPGR 12 years ago, great advancements have been achieved in the collection, conservation and utilisation of genetic resources" (IBPGR, 1987).

The above seems to be positive and useful for the Third World. However, there are still a series of questions which been raised on IBPGR, and which have to be analysed.

IBPGR priorities in the collection of genetic resources do not necessarily correspond to those of the Third World. Reviewing the priorities of IBPGR (Table III.1), it can be seen that most of the genetic resources considered to be of first priority are crops which are of importance to the industrialised countries. In the case of Central America, specifically Mexico, Guatemala, El Salvador, Honduras, Nicaragua and Costa Rica, even though the region has first priority as a centre of origin, the crops of importance for the population of that zone have quite low priorities for IBPGR:

First priority: *Phaseolus spp.*
Second priority: peanuts, cassava, potatoes, sweet
potato, cotton, American oil palm.
Third priority: maize, long beans, sunflower
and *Cajanus sp.*

When one compares these priorities with Table III.2, with the exception of maize, beans and cotton, none of these priority species are of great importance to the Central American people. This is mainly because few of the species commercially important for Central America are native to the region, but also because some of the regionally important native plants are not important internationally, as would be the case for pepper (*Capsicum spp.*) and some tropical fruit trees.

Of the over 130,000 samples collected through IBPGR funding over the last 12 years, there is a large amount of

Table III.2 The main crops of Mesoamerica, by production (1986)

Crop	Origin of the species	Mesoamerica		Industrialized Countries	
		Surface (1000 of Hectares)	Yield (Kg per Ha.)	Surface (1000 of Hectares)	Yield (Kg per Ha.)
Maize	Native	8698	1645	50478	5414
Sugarcane	Introduced	2620	55733	860	78833
Dry beans	Native	2055	653	2239	1007
Sorghum	Introduced	1964	2828	6476	3324
Green coffee	Introduced	1498	629	1	976
Wheat	Introduced	771	3656	138818	2059
Unhulled rice	Introduced	733	2981	4843	5247
Cotton	Native	706	2625	8995	2088
Safflower	Introduced	445	1102	162	1000
Sesame	Introduced	307	594	6	505
Soyabean	Introduced	306	1907	29398	1935
Barley	Introduced	281	1744	64574	2101
Cocoa grains	Native	231	389	0	-
Chickpea	Introduced	195	1090	162	626
Unhulled Peanuts	(Native)	173	1085	922	2176
Sisal	Native	163	598	0	1063
Sweet potato	Native	163	4643	134	15855
Cassava	Native	157	5447	0	-
Tomato	(Native)	145	14374	1104	28192

Crop	Status		10/1	10/1	
Jute and other fibres	Native	112		19	2587
Potatos	(Native)	112	12204	13451	15537
Dry Faba beans	Introduced	63	1250	369	1322
Chiles and peppers	Native	62	8632	184	14839
Yam	(Introduced)	57	5931	8	17827
Oats	Introduced	57	1104	24087	1684
Grapes	Introduced	49	10124	7605	6917
Melons	(Native)	34	11748	186	14408
Watermelon	Introduced	34	14874	708	12824
Squash	Native	32	7645	199	8371
Cucumber	Introduced	19	13467	423	14588
Cabbage	Introduced	18	9997	884	24591
Green peas	Introduced	16	3406	547	6958
Lentils	Introduced	15	831	220	858
Castor seed plant	Endemic	12	504	191	286
Dry onions	Introduced	11	6105	502	18389
Dry peas	Introduced	11	795	4644	1154
Green beans	Native	8	5304	221	6839
Garlic	Introduced	7	7302	100	5426
Carrots	Introduced	7	16398	331	23024
Sunflower seeds	Native	5	1259	8881	1244
Flax	Introduced	5	940	2398	484
Taro	(Native)	3	97881	31	14060
Rapeseed	Introduced	3	967	3872	1527
Cauliflower	Introduced	1	9855	163	16181
Eggplant	Introduced	1	28229	47	26998

Source: FAO (1987).

replicates (probably one-third) which are not in the Third World country where they were originally collected. They are instead being kept in the industrialised countries (Querol, 1986).

Due to its goals of helping interested institutions in their work with genetic resources, IBPGR has supported mainly conservation in industrialised countries and the creation of working standards. Still, there have been problems as IBPGR can be seen as an organisation ensuring, above all, the industrialised countries' access to the resources of the Third World (Mooney, 1983), which would lead to questions regarding its activities as a whole. At one point it was thought that a restructuring would happen within IBPGR to ensure its real support for the needs of the countries where genetic resources originated, but as this did not happen, the FAO Commission on Plant Genetic Resources had to be created.

3.2 The Plant Genetic Resources Commission of FAO

During the 22nd session of the FAO Conference in 1983, an International Undertaking on Plant Genetic Resources was agreed upon which made the following central propositions:

> "..... 5. Adherent governmental institutions which control plant genetic resources will follow the policy of allowing the exit of samples of those resources and will authorise their export, for the breeding of plants or for conservation of those resources. The samples will be handed out freely, based on exchange, or under those conditions which are jointly agreed on.
> 7.1 a) (The present international dispositions which institutions receiving fundings from IBPGR now follow will be adapted in order to ensure that) an international coordinated network of national, regional and international centres be developed, including an international network of base collections in genebanks under the auspices or the jurisdiction of FAO, which have assumed the responsibility of maintaining, for the benefit of the international community and applying

the principle of unrestricted exchange, base collection or active collections of plant genetic resources of certain plants species..."(FAO, 1985).

The countries which did not agree with this undertaking were: the Federal Republic of Germany, Canada, the United States of America, France, Japan, New Zealand, United Kingdom and Switzerland. The reason was that it included all types of plants as genetic resources, including breeders' lines and modern varieties, whereby those countries in which the main seeds corporations are established would have been forced to negotiate on an equal level with the countries which were centres of origin. Theoretically, the countries which signed the undertaking would not give genetic resources to the countries which did not sign it, as the second group of countries would not be accepting the idea of reciprocal responsibilities.

As the negotiating process was going to be a long one, a plant genetic resources commission was created, with the mandate to:

"... **1.** Watch over the execution of the agreement of the international undertaking on plant genetic resources;
2. Recommend the necessary or convenient measure to ensure that the global system be complete and its operation efficient in agreement with the undertaking and, particularly,
3. Examine all the matters relating to the policies, the programmes and the activities of FAO on the subject of plant genetic resources, and advise (various committees)" (FAO, 1983).

The IBPGR reacted to the existence of this Commission (in which all the countries of the world are represented, thereby creating a Third World majority), by saying: "IBPGR cannot operate at the same time under the authority of the CGIAR which created it and of which IBPGR is an integrated member and under the monitoring of the Commission, if this implies whatsoever kind of control. The IBPGR considers that the FAO undertaking includes aspects which go beyond the generally accepted concept of genetic resources as it includes breeders' lines (among those genetic resources to be freely exchanged)" (FAO, 1985). With these statements, IBPGR very clearly revealed itself as being quite concerned with ensuring that the investment of CGIAR be really used for the benefit of the investors.

In October of 1987, the Director-General of FAO confirmed the creation of an International Fund of Plant Genetic Resources, which through FAO must serve to do what IBPGR have not done in the areas of conservation and utilisation of genetic resources. This fund would obtain its financial resources from the money handed in by the main users of genetic resources: industrialised countries, and more specifically the seeds corporations. It is understood that this is a small compensation by the seeds industry, for utilising freely the resource without which they could not exist. A contribution of 1% of the sales price of modern-bred seeds in the world would allow the fund to work with approximately US$200 - $500 million a year.

Until now, industrialised countries have refused to contribute any money to the fund and continue to receive freely genetic resources from the Third World. Once again we see the absurdity of the poor subsidising the rich.

Collecting vehicle after two days of work.

IV
Collecting

WHOEVER WORKS ON GENETIC RESOURCES should theoretically dedicate himself only to collect and preserve the material. However, it is necessary to determine if the potential of each species justifies its systematic collecting. This decision should be taken in coordination with other institutions which evaluate potential genetic resources or, if such an institution does not exist, this analysis should be part of the genetic resources work.

1. IS IT NECESSARY TO COLLECT?

A plant species is considered to be useful based on the factors mentioned in the previous chapter and on the immediate needs of the breeding programme or the urgency to preserve that material from disappearing. A person interested in a certain genetic material will look for it in a genebank which has already collected that species. Alternatively, he will look for it in another country if it is a species whose centre of origin is not his own country. If the previous alternatives do not yield a result, he will go to collect the material in the field.

When one speaks of species whose preservation is needed ("endangered species"), a series of factors should be considered. It is necessary to determine how urgently collection is needed in order to preserve it. In the case of *Amaranthus*, a widely distributed weed in Mexico, it would be useless to collect it, unless a direct programme of utilisation exists, as its wide distribution ensures that it will survive as a species, and even all sub-races will prevail in Mexico. There are however other species which necessitate collection:

a) Species which have been over-exploited and whose population density is low.

This case is exemplified by the red cedar (*Cedrella odorata L.*) in the Lacandone jungle in the South East of Mexico. For many years, the Lacandone jungle logging company exploited the areas with a high concentration of cedars. Paths were opened which were directed specifically to those populations, with secondary paths towards each tree. As a result, not only the desired tree was taken out, but all the trees which formed the micro-population of the zone. Other useful trees were simply destroyed. Such a systematic exploitation of the resource could result in its destruction.

Nowadays there are fewer and fewer cedar trees of good quality in the Lacandone jungle. The reforestation programmes promoted by the Mexican government over the last few years have not had the success which was expected. The low competition conditions needed to ensure the survival of the small trees causes them to develop an irregular pattern generally with branching at the lower parts of the tree, which makes them useless for timber. Therefore, it is urgent to collect cedar seeds. These seeds, however, have a very low storage tolerance. Seeds collected in 1980 by the author, which at the time of collection had 97% germination, had gone down to 56% germination three months later. Therefore, it is necessary to maintain this species as developed trees. The problem which arises is how and where to store hundreds of cedar trees.

This example gets complicated if a joint programme of collection and storage is expected. Since the Lacandone jungle is a biosphere reserve and the patrimony of humanity according to the law, it would therefore be the ideal place to maintain the populations of red cedar. But this same jungle has been used as a "political reserve" to resettle peasants of other areas of Mexico who were claiming land and to whom one could not (or one did not want to) give land in their states of origin. The problem is not only a technical one but also has political implications.

b) Traditional maize in Mexico should be collected for two reasons: on one hand, the need for traditional maize for breeding programmes and, on the other hand, the replacement of this maize by the introduction of modern-bred varieties. Currently, there is a good availability of maize germplasm which has been stored in the maize genebank in Mexico City. However, not all of the potential tropical maize sources have been obtained (Hernandez X., Personal Communication).

The Agricultural Development Bank in Mexico presently extends credit only to those peasants who plant modern-bred varieties. The consequence may be positive as some of the modern maize varieties yield more than the traditional ones, in a shorter time. However, many of the traditional varieties which have been replaced by a hybrid or any other modern variety, disappear in the process.

Although in the case of maize in Mexico the problem is not yet a general one, in India and Pakistan the introduction of semi-dwarf wheat as part of the "Green Revolution" has eliminated traditional varieties altogether in the areas concerned. Semi-dwarf wheat had good characteristics for Indian conditions, but they used large amounts of energy, fertiliser and pesticides, and when oil prices went up as from 1972, the cost of inputs increased considerably, too. The Indian government did not have the economic capacity to continue subsidising fertilisers, so the introduced varieties had to be planted without fertilisers or pesticides. This caused a significant reduction in the yields, much below the level of traditional varieties. The peasants tried to go back to traditional varieties but these did not exist anymore, or at least they did not have the seeds.

If the material and the natural conditions are not at risk of being destroyed for some time, it is possible to do *in situ* conservation. This conservation technique involve the continued growth of the material in the wild or under cultivated conditions, assuming that the environment will remain balanced and unchanged. Then it is not necessary to collect the material.

2. PREVIOUS DETERMINATIONS

Once it has been established whether it is necessary to collect, one must determine the characteristics of the collection, the limitations which one may find in the field and the planning of the collecting trip.

One can define two main types of collecting trips: trips for specific crops and collecting trips according to ecological zones. The first kind of trip generally corresponds to the search for plants of a species with outstanding characteristics, and will therefore disregard species which do not correspond to this specific interest of a programme. This type of collecting trip (monocrop) is in line with a specialisation philosophy but not as efficient as the collecting trip by ecological zone (multicrop).

The second type of trip includes in its objective the description and collection of ecological variability which, in the typical case of multicrop cultivation of the Third World, corresponds not only to an effort to maintain the information of associated species for their breeding, but also allows studies on co-evolution to be made and efforts to develop agriculture on the technical bases of production which the peasant uses in reality.

Creech (1970) differentiates between collecting trips for breeding programmes and collecting trips looking for new crop alternatives. In the case of collection for breeding programmes, specialised researchers collect plants with resistance to diseases and other special characteristics. It is recommended that specialists on the crop under study and its diseases be included. In the case of the search for new crops, the group of collectors should include an ethnobotanist and people with wide knowledge of the utilised species in the collection zone.

Hernandez X. (1978) presents an abstract of the

ethnobotanical exploration postulates which are as follows:
–   There is always background information on the area to be explored, in time, environment and culture.
–   There is a close relationship between the ecological environment and the development of cultivated plants and useful spontaneous plants.
–   Man has been and is the most important defining factor on the nature of the crops and the process of production.
–   Each species and variant thereof has distinct morphological characteristics and ecological adaptations.
–   The knowledge accumulated over thousands of years takes time to be recovered.
–   Exploration must be a periodical and continuous process building on better knowledge and more precision at each stage.

For the analysis about the ease and possibility of a collecting trip, the following methods based on the one used by the Royal Botanical Gardens at Kew, is proposed (Thompson, 1979a).
Five factors should be studied when a proposal is made. Each factor has four levels, the first one being the most appropriate or easiest one. If in any one of the factors one can find a high level of difficulty, the collecting trip should be reconsidered. The criteria for the evaluation of a collecting trip are:

a.   Priority
i)   Crop or plant of priority for the country, with present importance and immediate utilisation possibilities. Area of known variability should need an urgent intervention due to erosion risks.
ii)   Crop or plant of priority of the country, with potential importance, or crop of present importance for other countries. Area of potential variability.
iii)   Crop or plant of potential non-studied use and with known uses. Non-studied ecological zone. Trip to complement variability which is already available from the area or to obtain limited variability.

iv)   Secondary crop or plant with no probable concrete objectives in its use. Widely collected ecological zone. Material available in other genebanks.

b.   Biology
i)   The life cycle of a plant has been widely studied or is well known. Existing information about flowering period and seed formation is abundant.
ii)   There is indicative information about the fruiting season and seeds production season, either directly or through reference to similar species in similar habitats.
iii)   Flowering and fruit production season in doubt; little information available as reference.
iv)   Little or no information available to indicate timing or frequency of fruit or seed production.

c.   Accessibility
i)   Population easily accessible. Seeds develop at a reasonable distance from the ground. Synchronic or profuse ripening.
ii)   Population accessible by conventional transportation means. Seeds available in adequate quantities without need for sophisticated equipment.
iii)   Population accessible only through special transportation means, or seed in small quantities, or seed which needs special collection techniques (difficult access; very big trees with fruits in the higher parts).
iv)   Population almost inaccesible or individuals hard to find. Zones where risks to the life of the collector exist. Seed which grows isolated or is almost impossible to collect without special equipment (certain plants growing on perpendicular rocks walls).

d.   Reaction to storage
i)   Seed can be stored under typical conditions. Reacts positively to low temperatures and low humidity.
ii)   Seed which can probably be stored for long periods of time based on an analogy with other species of the same genera.

iii) Seed probably not adequate for long term storage or which needs special storage techniques. Plants of vegetative reproduction.

iv) Seed known not to survive for long periods under storage, absence of methods to extend viability.

e. Regeneration Potential

i) Plants which can be easily cultivated, quick maturing (annuals), with abundant seeds production. Frequently self-pollinated (autogamous) species.

ii) Seeds easily obtainable under cultivation, in sufficient quantity, over a short time (annuals). It is necessary to use special cultivation techniques. Frequently cross-pollinated (alogamous) species.

iii) Seeds are difficult to obtain in adequate quantities or only after long periods (perennials).

iv) Adequate seed quantities are almost impossible to obtain or only after exceedingly long periods (*Agave sp.*).

As a first example of the use of this method, we will evaluate the proposal to collect traditional maize in the North of Nicaragua (Figure IV.1). Maize is of high priority in Nicaragua as it is the main staple crop. Even though the biological cycle of maize is known in general, there is no specific information available as to the dates of planting and harvest. It is necessary to review bibliography and talk with people who know the area in order to get there at the time when seed is available. The access to the North of Nicaragua is limited due to the presence of terrorist groups ("contras") who enter the country from Honduras and frequently attack civilians. The collectors would risk their lives if they worked in the area. When contra activities stop, access will be very easy. There are, on the other hand, certain areas of interest for collection which need special transportation which will prolong the length of the collecting trip. The reaction to storage as well as the regeneration techniques are known and present no limitations.

Based on these parameters, one can establish a final

FIGURE IV.1   PROPOSAL OF A COLLECTION TRIP FOR STAPLE GRAINS IN THE NORTH OF NICARAGUA.

COLLECTION TRIP TO: North of Nicaragua
CROP OR SPECIES: Staple grains
PROPOSED DATE: 1987
DURATION OF TRIP: 3 weeks

CRITERIA	LEVEL OF DIFFICULTY			
	NULL (1)	LOW (2)	MEDIUM (3)	HIGH (4)
Priority	XX			
Biology	XX			
Access				XX
Storage	XX			
Regeneration	XX			

General classification of the trip: 8/25

For future execution

mark of three, for maximum difficulty of 15 (3/15). The proposal is possible and important, but it cannot be done while the access problem is not solved.

As a second example, we take a proposal to collect species from the genera *Anona* in the forest of Madre de Dios in Peru (Figure IV.2). The biological cycle is not sufficiently known to ensure the timing for maximum seed availability. Access is very difficult as isolated communities in Madre de Dios very often have no land access and one needs either river or air transportation. Reaction to storage is known due to studies made in the case of *A. cherimoya* L. and *A. muricata* L., which prove that seeds will lose viability very quickly under conventional storage condition with low humidity and low temperature (Roberts and King, 1981). The cultivation of the species is easy. However, the problem of regeneration of seeds resides in the long reproductive cycle of a plant (three to four years from planting to fruit production). On the other hand, the utilisation of germplasm will be more adequate if vegetative parts are collected for the conservation of outstanding qualities. This would need adequate collecting equipment.

Based on these classification factors, one can reach a final mark of 9/15, whereby the proposal is not acceptable under present conditions. A more detailed analysis of taxonomy and alternative storage means, as for example the creation of a collecting garden or a varietal garden, is necessary.

Various authors consider the need to take into account other factors in the preparation of collecting trips. For example, Bunting and Kuckuck (1970) consider:

a. Physical factors: geography, geology, climate, soil and length of agricultural cycle. All these factors can be studied through bibliographical reviews and the study of maps and climatic data.
b. Ecological, human and historic factors, agricultural systems and information on the crops in the zones where the collecting trip will take place.

FIGURE IV.2   PROPOSAL OF A COLLECTING TRIP FOR ANONACEAE IN MADRE DE DIOS, PERU.

COLLECTION TRIP TO: Madre de Dios
CROP OR SPECIES: *Anona*
PROPOSED DATE:
DURATION OF TRIP:

CRITERIA	LEVEL OF DIFFICULTY			
	NULL (1)	LOW (2)	MEDIUM (3)	HIGH (4)
Priority			XX	
Biology		XX		
Access			XX	
Storage			XX	
Regeneration			XX	

General classification of the trip: 14/25   Limiting factors should be solved before the trip can be made.

A search of information is made at regional level, including information of zones which were not initially planned for collecting, but which could get to be studied. It is important to have a notion of the whole of the region, in order to be able to work with more clarity and more detail during the trip itself.

It is necessary to make sure an institution exists which will be willing to maintain the collected material. Timothy and Goodman (1979) describe the real problems which arise with the management of genetic resources, taking maize as an example. Materials which were collected in different parts of America over the last 30 years, have   disappeared on occasions and in other cases have not been adequately preserved, not even in an international agricultural research centre like CIMMYT. This is due to the lack of a continuous policy for the preservation of genetic resources of maize and to other human errors. Collecting is not enough if there is no organised infrastructure ready to preserve the results of that collection.

The specific preparation of the collecting trip has been widely discussed (Bennett, 1970; Schuze-Kraft, 1979a; Arora, 1981). Once the itinerary and specific goals of a collecting trip have been defined, a team of collectors must be organized, with few people, in order to allow a good reception by the peasants in the collecting area. Under ideal conditions, the working team should be made up of two or three people. Should there be much interest in participating in the collecting trip, the most adequate procedure is to subdivide the team and   create sub-teams. During the collecting activities, the sub-groups will work independently and will have coordinating meetings at the end of each day. These meetings will allow the team to organize the collected data and samples, complement information on taxonomy and on variability in the collected zone in order to enlarge or reduce the collecting activities the next day.

The length of a collecting trip will depend on the availability of economic resources. Collecting trips in the past lasted from three to six months (Hawkes, 1941). Nowadays one can make an efficient trip in 15 to 45 days. The material

TABLE IV.I MATERIALS FOR GENETIC RESOURCES COLLECTING TRIPS

1. Scientific equipment
* Pocket altimeter
* Compass
  Binoculars
* Camera (if possible with a wide lens (30mm) & telephoto
* Sufficient films

  optional:
  Tape recorder and blank tapes
  Hygrometer
  Soil thermometer
  Maximum and minimum thermometer
  Soil sampling equipment

2. Collection Gear
  (for live plant materials):
* Collecting sheets
* Plastic Bags in different sizes
* Paper bags in different sizes
  Cloth bags in different sizes
* Adhesive and hanging tags
  Field books
* Waterproof and wax markers
* Strings and ropes
* Scissors
* Bottles with wide openings
* Tape
* Stapler and staples
* Pencils and erasers
* Shovels
* Gardener's scissors
* Grafting knife

  (for herbarium samples and pests):
* Press
* Newspaper
* Cardboard
* Formalin solution for succulent plants

* Insecticide
Container for nodules
Net for insect capture
Bottles to keep pests

(for the processing of seeds):
mesh cage for the drying of paper bags
boxes to thresh and clean the seeds ·

3. Additional recommended equipment:
Portable refrigerator for vegetative material
Dryer (Temperature obtained with an alcohol burner or with a generator and light bulbs)

4. Transport equipment:
* Four wheel drive vehicle, with low pressure tyres with tube, grill and compartments for equipment and collections

Spare parts:
* It is absolutely necessary to take a fan-belt, tools for tire repair, air pump, pressure gauge, spare tanks with gasoline, oil, full tool set, spare tyres and water (very important).

Adaptations to the vehicle recommended by Bennet (1970) are:
a) Power wrench moved by the motor, with steel cable, to pull the car out when it has lost traction
b) inside lights in the different parts of the vehicle to allow work while driving, or during stops.

5. Published materials
* Maps of the highest resolution of the collection area
Climatic, geological and ecological maps
Road maps with information on the possible gasoline and oil supply points, sleeping quarters, medical services   and post and telephone offices (tourist maps often contain this information)
Taxonomic keys of the species to be collected
Descriptions of the flora of the area
Dictionaries of the dialects or languages of the zone
Short history of the zone (cultures, habits, religions)

6. **Miscellaneous personal equipment:**
   High, water resistant boots
   Water containers (50 L) and water bottles
   Material for personal hygiene
   Enough clothing if it rains
   Plastic bags
   Watch
   Candles
* Swiss-type knifes to solve everything else
* Letters of introduction

7. **Medical supplies**
   Vaccines
* Water purifying tablets (Chlorine)
   Antidiarrheaics
* Antihistamine (allergies)
   Methiolate or alcohol (small wounds)
   Antibiotics (infections)
* Anagelsics(painkiller)
   Antimalarial tablets (quinine)
   Liophylised anti-snake serum
   Disposable syringes
   Cotton, bandages and gauze
* Mosquito repellent

8. **Camping equipment:**
   Tent
   Hammocks and/or sleeping bags with mosquito nets
* Flashlights
* Enough batteries
   Stove and cooking equipment (Don't forget the fuel)
* Matches

Note: those preceeded by asterisks are essential and indispensible.

and maximum equipment for a collecting trip is described in Table IV.1, even though under real conditions one can collect with significantly less equipment than is described here.

3. COLLECTING METHODS

Once the species with which one is going to work have been defined, the team established and the timing and routes determined, one of the important remaining issues is to establish the data which will be taken in the field.

Each collector, in different times and places, has generated a list of variables he would like to take as passport information. Passport information is obtained during the collecting trip, and includes information on the place of collection, the visible variability of the samples collected and other general information. They include also the scientific and common names of the collected species. The unique accession number is only assigned at the time the sample gets to the genebank.

In order to standardise the information at an international level, IBPGR and FAO have proposed a series of passport descriptors. Based on these and with some additions, the Genebank of Native Species in Chapingo, Mexico designed a unique collecting sheet (Figure IV.3), which should serve to make collections for breeding programmes, and of potential species as well as wild species. The collecting sheets, printed on opaque cardboard in order to avoid reflection on sunny days has a continuous numbering printed on it, in order to avoid confusion once the material gets to the bank. In the lower part of the collecting sheet there are three tabs which can be ripped off, with the same sheet number which are used the following way: one is introduced inside the bag, one outside of the bag and the third one is used for the herbarium sample. The use of this sheet is simplified by the use of a manual (Appendix II). This sheet has been adapted by the national programmes in Nicaragua and Peru.

The collecting sheet has 71 descriptors: some of these

Figure IV.3a Genetic Resources Collecting Sheet

Date of collection

Y Y M M D D

Accession number

Sheet number

1 2 7 1

I. Taxonomy

Family

Genus

Species

Subspecies

Variety

Common name

Local name

II. Geography

Name of the collection

Place of collection

Municipality of collection

State of collection

Country of collection

Latitude

Longitude

Altitude (metres a. sea)

III. Ecology

15) Physiography

1. Level
2. Top of mountain
3. Steep slope
4. Rounded top
5. Strong slope
6. Medium slope
7. Terrace
8. Light slope

16) Description of the site

1. Field
2. Roadside
3. Freshwater shore
4. Swamp
5. Seashore
6. Desert
7. Pasture land
8. Wood

17) Type of soil

1. Sandy
2. Lime
3. Clay
4. Organic
5. Stony
6. Other

18) Shadiness

1. Sunny
2. Partly shaded
3. Shaded
4. Other

3. Evergreen wood
10. Low tropical forest
11. Medium tropical forest
12. High tropical forest t
13. Garden
14. Family garden
15. Other

IV. Characteristics of the material

19) Growth conditions

1. Wild
2. Tolerated
3. Encouraged
4. Cultivated

20) Growth Habit

1. Crawling
2. Herbaceous
3. Bushy
4. Tree
5. Epiphitic
6. Water growing
7. Climbing
8. Other

21) Abundancy

1. Very scarce
2. Scarce
3. Not very frequent
4. Frequent
5. Very frequent
6. Solid population

22) Variability of the population

1. Homogeneous
   (100% uniform)
2. Little variability
   (variability is not very visible)
3. Heterogenous
4. Very heterogenous
5. Could not be determined

Note:In cases 3, 4 and 5
various samples should be taken

23) Biological Cycle

1. Spring annual
2. Intermediate annual
3. Winter annual
4. Biannual
5. Short-lived Perennial (2 - 5 years)
6. Medium-lived Perennial (6 to 15 years)
7. Long-lived Perennial (16 to 50 years)
8. Very long lived Perennial (over 50 years)
9. Unknown

24) Reproductive Mechanism

1. Asexual (Vegetative)
2. Through seed
3. Both

25) Type of Material

1. Native species in wild state
2. Native variety
3. Special non-cultivated material
4. Modern bred variety
5. Other variety (introduced, obsolete, etc.)
6. Unknown

Sheet Number 1271

Name of the collection

Sheet Number 1271

Name of the collection

Sheet Number 1271

Name of the collection

Sheet Number 1271

Name of the collection

Figure IV.3b

V The Informant

Name

27) Activity
1. Peasant
2. Biologist
3. Breeder, agricultural engineer
4. Medicine man, witch doctor
5. Doctor
6. Inhabitant

28) Characteristics
1. Not a peasant
2. Small peasant
3. Medium peasant
4. Farmer or landlord

29) Land Property
1. Collective Property
2. Individual Property
3. Rented land
4. Others

30) Relationship Between Production and the Market
1. Consumed (direct use)
2. Mixed
3. 100% commercial

VI. The Crop

31) Planting date
32) Harvest date
33) Second planting date
34) Second harvest date

Y Y M M D D

35) Amount of seed used (kg. per hectare)
36) Yield (kg. per hectare)
37) Relationship Between Production and the Market
1. Consumed (direct use)
2. Mixed
3. 100% commercial

VII. Utilisation

38) Main use — Part of the plant
39) Secondary use — Part of the Plant
40) Specific use and way of use

Uses
1. Food source
2. Medicinal
3. Industrial
4. Fodder crop
5. Ornamental
6. Ceremonial
7. Weed
8. None
9. Others

Parts of the Plant
1. Seed
2. Flower
3. Fruit
4. Stem
5. Leaf
6. Root
7. Tuber
8. Bark
9. The whole plant
10. None
11. Other

VIII. The Collection

41) Type of collected material
1. Seed
4. Cutting

42) Type of Collection
1. Field
4. Peasants store

43) Age of the sample

44) Sampling method ☐

1. Random
2. Best according to the informant
3. Best according to the collector
4. Worst according to the informant
5. Worst according to the collector
6. Other

45) Amount collected ☐

Units ☐

1. Seeds
2. Grains
3. Fruits
4. Plants
5. Spikes
6. Tubers
7. Ears
8. Cuttings
9. Grams
10. Kilograms
11. Measures
12. Others

46) Herbarium specimen ☐

1. yes   2. no

47) Photograph ☐

1 yes
2 no

Number of roll ☐☐☐☐

Number of shot ☐☐☐☐

IX. Associated collections

	Sheet Number	Accession number	Type of Association	Types of Association
48)	☐☐☐☐	☐☐☐☐	☐	1. Multiple samples due to heterogenity
49)	☐☐☐☐	☐☐☐☐	☐	2. Main crop
50)	☐☐☐☐	☐☐☐☐	☐	3. Crop associated to this collection
51)	☐☐☐☐	☐☐☐☐	☐	4. Weed of this collection
				5. Ecosystem
				6. Other

X. Supplemental information

52) Notes ☐☐☐☐☐☐☐☐☐☐☐☐☐☐☐☐

53) Name of the collector ☐☐☐☐☐☐☐☐☐☐☐☐☐

54) Name of the taxonomic identifier ☐☐☐☐☐☐☐☐☐☐☐☐☐

Notes

are not for general use and need not be filled. However, it was considered necessary to include as many descriptors as possible, so that users with different objectives (collectors of medicinal plants, food plants, ecologists, etc.) could use the same sheet and then data would be introduced to the same computerised database in all cases.

When all the passport data has been taken, it is often necessary to generate an additional descriptors list to characterise the samples of each species, as will be seen in Chapter VII.

4. COLLECTION TECHNIQUES

It is necessary to collect the material and take the data in an orderly way. It is worth going through Leon (1974), who compiled information about tropical crop introduction techniques, including specific information on the management of material, even though frequently the comments are after the collecting work. In the following pages, we will look in detail at the data and material collecting techniques.

4.1 Data Collecting Techniques

The basic data on the collected material is introduced in the collecting sheet. Other useful data, which is not included in the collecting sheet should be written in a field notebook, in which general information will be kept in order to be able to link information from the collecting sheet, the collected material itself, photographs and other relevant information. In some cases it will not be possible to fill out the collecting sheet immediately and there will be meetings at the end of the day or as part of the final activities of the collecting trip. The field book will allow subsequent correction of mistakes observed during the collecting trip and the writing of the final report. The main objective of a collecting trip is to collect material, but it should also be used to establish future collecting trips and to propose research areas to be developed.

The final report of a collecting trip should include information on genetic erosion in the collected area, either due to agriculture (introduction of modern-bred varieties, new technologies), effects due to the environment (eruptions, droughts) or through badly designed "development" programmes (oil fields, roads). This report will also include a full description of the physiography and vegetation of the area visited, contacts with people, material which was not collected but was outstanding or highly variable, recommendation of collecting dates for species which did not have seeds or propagative material during this trip and any other information which allows future collecting expeditions to be improved.

4.2 Techniques for the Collection of Material

The collecting of genetic resources, as opposed to botanical collections, searches for maximum variability and the material to propagate this variability, and not only specimen plants. The collector tries to obtain this variability and must follow an organised plan in order to get the maximum genetic information in the shortest possible time.

Genetic variability in a population is determined by the presence of different alleles for the same *locus*. Each one of these alleles will have a specific frequency in a given population, with some *loci* showing a great variability and others with only two different alleles.

It is easy to detect and collect variability in those cases where genes have a qualitative phenotypic expression. Most of the genes have an additive or epistatic expression, which makes it difficult to detect them visually. In that case, one can use the limits recommended by Chandel (1981), who defines two groups of allelic distribution:

1. Common alleles or variants of high frequency: (Probability greater than 5%, generally less than four alleles per locus).
   In most populations, this is the main type of variants and sampling is easy. Even if one were to collect only 40 independent genomes (seeds, stems, or tubers from

different plants), it is quite probable that these alleles would be included.

2. Alleles of wide distribution, with low frequency:
(Probability less than 5%, generally more than four alleles per locus)
The sampling of these alleles implies collecting work of more intense and systematic type. It is necessary to know the distribution of these alleles within the collecting sites. In general, the determining factor for their inclusion in the sample will be the size of the sample and the sampling technique.

One of the determining factors of variability is the means and the type of reproduction of the plant. In the case of self-pollinated (autogamous) species, there is less variability than in the case of cross-pollinated (alogamous) species. This leads to the definition of the alogamous as a social population and the autogamous as the individualist population. The generalisation of this definition is based on the fact that the main factor for the variability of population is the size of its reproductive unit, which is a function of the number and density of plants in the place of collection, the type of reproduction of the plant and dispersion and amount of pollen and seed (Chandel, 1981).

Allard (1970a) doubts whether in the case of autogamous species, there is much homogeneity. In most in-depth studies on autogamous species in the wild, one can detect that there is not only a great polymorphism, but also that it is frequent to find heterozygous plants, which later segregate.

On top of the variability within the population, one must consider the variability between populations in the collected area. For Allard (1970a), geographic distribution influences most of the variability collected. This variability presents itself at two levels. On the first level, variability is due to the presence or absence of certain alleles in specific geographical zones. For example, in the barley collection of the United States Department of Agriculture, 75% of the accessions which are resistant to net-blotch come from Manchuria, even though only 12% of the total collection comes from that area.

At the second level — within a geographical zone — the variability will be determined by the microclimates and changes in soil and other environmental factors. Following the example by Allard in the case of wild oats (*Avena fatua*), differences which can be observed between populations due to changes in altitude and humidity in a few kilometres are equivalent to the differences due to much greater changes in latitude. A difference of a few kilometres in an east-west transect (from the coast towards the Sierra Nevada in California) gave a difference of two weeks in the time (days) taken for flowering. That same difference of two weeks in the north-south transect can be found only with a distance of 800 kilometres.

Where distances are smaller (less than 100 metres), it can be supposed that the intensity of changes will also be smaller. However, small changes in the environment can lead to great changes in genotype, in alogamous as well as autogamous species. The autogamous species may evolve divergently due to differences in stoniness, drainage, or any other environmental factors. Also, in the case of alogamous species one can detect abrupt changes at small distances. *Agrostis tenuis*, an alogamous grass which is self-incompatible, i.e. it cannot fertilise itself, has developed resistance to heavy metal toxicity close to a mine, and the transition between the individuals of the population which are tolerant and those which are not, can be seen in fewer than 20 metres.

In the collecting process, there are two main sampling mechanisms:

1) **Random sampling**, where there is no bias and one tries to get the sample to represent the original population. The advantage of this way of collecting is that it allows one to obtain a sub-population which will behave in a similar manner to the original population. The disadvantage can be seen in the loss of the elements with low frequencies ('rare' alleles or individuals) in

the original population; that is to say those which are to be found at the extremes of the distribution curve.

2) Biased sampling, which allows one to collect visible alleles, even with low frequencies. In this case, one tries to preserve that information which would not normally be included in a random sampling, unless a very large sample — which in practice would be impossible to manage — had been collected. This technique has the advantage of ensuring the presence of those alleles (whose expression is visible) with low frequencies, but it creates an artificial population which is not balanced and does not represent the original population.

The random sampling has a type error S

$$S = \frac{\sigma}{\sqrt{n}}$$

where σ is the standard deviation of the population for that character, and n is the number of collected individuals.

In the case of finite population samples, Bennet (1970) proposes a change in the previous equation to:

$$S = \frac{\sigma}{\sqrt{n}} \sqrt{1-f}$$

where f is the fraction of the general population which is included in the sample. Generally, as the fraction of the original population from which the sample was taken is small, this term is not significant. From what was just said, one can deduce that the sample must be big in the case where the population has a large variability and when the original population is small, it is easy to reduce sampling error by increasing the size of the sample (n).

When one collects in the field (as opposed to collection in farmers' storage or markets), the strategy to follow is to initially cover as large an area as possible. The area where one wants to do a collection is divided into squares, looking for maximum homogeneity within each element or space in the grid. This will depend on the variability in the collecting zone, as much due to environmental characteristics as to the social and economic conditions.

In the case of a species which can be found from 200 up to 2,500 metres above sea level in the collecting area, the grid would be determined mainly by the level curves. If various ethnic groups cultivated species in the area, it is probable that each one of them will have a different variant from the others and therefore the grids will correspond to ethnic areas. The junction of both elements of information will generate a grid which will most adequately determine the places where one should expect changes in the characteristics of the sampled material. In each grid, of course, samples should be taken.

In the second phase, one can collect with more specific goals and in a more intensive manner, even though practice shows that this rarely happens before 10 or 20 years have elapsed since the first collecting trip. The objectives of a tighter grid would be determined by the results of the evaluation of the material collected in the first trip. On the second trip, one would work with less accessible areas and collect more in those squares where interesting variability is found.

In the case of samples in the market places, which are very frequently convenient, it is necessary to know the origin of the material one is collecting. Even though it is true that it is easy to work this way, what one observes in the market does not necessarily represent the seeds of the peasants. There is a possibility that seeds of modern-bred varieties which are degenerating (segregating in the case of hybrids) are being collected. The seed stores or granaries are an excellent source of genetic material, because, as opposed to what happens in the case of a market, one can be certain of collecting what the producer uses.

The family orchards are a third source and if the variability is not large due to the small size of the plant population, one can consider a series of family orchards in a village as one sampling unit.

4.2.1   Non-tree species reproduced by seeds

The sampling unit will be the peasant's field, his granary, or in the case of wild species, a unit of surface defined on the basis of the variability of the population. The sampling surface for each collection will be smaller as one sees or expects more variability. It is important to take seeds from different plants, as otherwise one loses 50% of the alleles (Querol, 1982b). In all cases, one should start with a random sample taking a small number of seeds per plant (10 - 50) and trying to sample 50 to 100 plants according to Hawkes (1980) and 200 to 500 plants according to Bennett (1970). This will lead to a range of between 500 and 25,000 seeds. Table IV.2 shows an abstract of a proposal by Hawkes (1980) on the amount of seeds needed. K. L. Tao (Personal Communication), responsible for the seed conservation area in IBPGR, makes the following proposal as to the use of seeds in the case of uniform (homogeneous) collections:

		Number of seeds
Initial viability test	=	400
Humidity test	=	200
Six viability tests during storage	=	1200
Two humidity determinations during storage	=	400
Three seed distributions	=	300
One regeneration	=	100
Accidents during tests or regeneration	=	400
Total	=	3,000 seeds

TABLE IV.2 AMOUNT OF SEEDS FOR THE COLLECTION AND CONSERVATION OF GENETIC RESOURCES
Taken from Hawkes (1980)

Type of population	For Collecting	For base collection	For collection duplicate	For active collection	Total for storage
Very variable (heteroge- neous)	5000 (100 plants, 50 seeds from each plant)	12000	3000	5000	20000 (1)
Quite uniform (homoge- neous)	2500 (50 plants, 50 seeds each plant)	4000	1000	3000	8000

(1) Due to storage limitations, sometimes only a total of 12,000 seeds, and not 20,000 are stored in the case of heterogenous populations.

This is adequate if one supposes that a hundred seeds would be good enough for regeneration and that this material will be used mainly for long term storage. It is preferable to increase the sample size to 4,000 in order to have asecurity range. In the case of variable (heterogeneous) collections, the sample size increases to 12,000 seeds. It should be clear that these figures correspond to theoretical proposals, and that in practice, collections are almost always much smaller. On top of that, it is not logical to use more than half of the sample to make internal tests in the genebank.

If one finds interesting variants, it is recommended that a second (or various) biased sample be taken, which will be treated as different collections, keeping the information which links them to the random sample on the collecting sheets.

There are two special cases which occur frequently:

a) There is not enough material. One then collects what is available, considering in this case that if the species is in danger of extinction, it is important not to be the cause, in an effort to preserve the species, of its disappearance in the wild state.

b) Variability is very wide. The collection of maize in traditional fields in Latin America is a typical case. Independent samples will be made of groups of plants in similar places, otherwise one will increase the sample size.

The processing of the material in the fields includes drying, and if absolutely necessary only, treatment with fungicide or insecticide. One should avoid all kinds of treatment which can reduce the long-term viability of the seeds. The treatment will be applied only after the seed has been dried in order not to damage the embryo.

If the collected species has seeds inside fleshy fruits, they must be extracted, washed, sometimes fermented, and dried **during** the trip. Otherwise, the fruits may rot, with consequent damage to the seeds. Seeds should be dried during the nights, and should the drying process not be completed, it should be finished the next day, taking care never to store seeds with a very high humidity content in plastic bags. Miguel Holle (Personal Communication) proposes the "hygienic method" which consists of depositing on toilet paper the seeds of each fruit. On top of the fast drying rate of the seeds, this allows for the maintainence of the order of samples, and controls the origin of each seed by fruit and plant.

4.2.2. Vegetatively Reproduced Species (roots and tubers)

This type of collections is more complex, due to the collecting and storage problems. During the collecting trip, the following problems may arise:

Frequently, there is no security in collecting different genotypes, unless the part of the plant above the ground is alive, and if it is, generally, the tubers or reproductive parts will not be ready for harvest. It is recommended not to collect more than one propagule for every 10-15 neighbouring plants, and to try to collect in a wide area.

Due to their structure, most of the propagules are easily attacked by bacteria and fungi and if they are dried excessively they can die from dehydration. It is recommended to wash the propagules thoroughly with a diluted fungicide solution (Arasan, 5 g/L) and to keep them in the freshest part of the collecting vehicle, in a saw-dust filled container (Hawkes, 1941).

It takes a while to collect roots and tubers as very often one has to dig deeply, down to 1 metre in the case of *Dioscorea*. The size of the propagules can be big (*Musa sp.*, *Colocasia sp.*). It is recommended to look for smaller propagules because, evidently, their size will not change their same genetic information. If there is also sexual reproduction it is convenient to collect botanical seeds. Even though it may not have the alleles combination of the mother plants, it will have the alleles as such.

The storage of this type of collections is only possible in collecting gardens, or with tissue culture techniques, which will be looked at in Chapter VI. It is absolutely necessary, at the time one leaves for a collecting trip, to be sure of the availability of land and personnel for the preservation of the collected material.

Thomas (1981) proposes the following methods to collect cultivated species with vegetative reproduction:

a)   Sample each distinct morphotype within the populations.

b)   Repeat the sampling every so often. The frequency of those samples will depend on the diversity of the environment, distribution and density of the members of the population and the frequency of the new phenotypic (visible) forms. The collection intensity

(number of plant sampled) will depend on the variability at the sampling locations.

c)   Try to find morphological characteristics in the part of
the plant above the ground which indicate characteristics also of the underground part in order to sample
more efficiently, for example the colour of the stem in
the cassava plant is associated with the external skin
colour of the root.

d)   Sample botanical seeds whenever possible. If the seeds
come from the same group of plants, consider it as only
one sample.

e)   The samples in one village and from various fields can
be mixed if the similarities in naming and morphology
are significant, but that would be better done later in
the genebank or collection garden.

4.2.3. Woody Species (Trees)

In the case of woody species, there are problems which arise
from the sampling as well as the collection itself. Their
preservation also has some peculiarities.

Woody species have, according to Sinha (1981), the
following significant characteristics:

a) Wide range of ecological growing conditions.
b) Frequent clonal propagation under cultivation.
c) Long life cycles.
d) Big size.

On top of that, the seeds of many trees are "recalcitrant", which means that they cannot be stored under typical
conditions (low temperature, low humidity content) without
a significant and sometimes even drastic loss of their viability.

An advantage, due to the length of their life cycle, is
that they are less susceptible to annual fluctuations of the
environment, which allows for a sampling of real variability.

Lastly, problems arise due to the need to maintain this
clonally propagated species in collection gardens. This im-

plies an area of land proportional to the number of samples, as multiple grafts are in risk of being eliminated during the growth of the grafting stock. It therefore becomes necessary to rationally reduce the number of samples based on the availability of land.

Hawkes (1980) and Sinha (1981) agree on differentiating techniques depending on whether they are wild or cultivated species:

a) Wild Species
Collect the seeds from 10 to 15 individuals in a maximum of 10 hectares. If the surface is larger, make separate collections. Collect the maximum possible seeds from each tree, and if no seeds are available, collect some vegetative part of each one of the sampled trees.
Sinha (1981) proposes a three phase collection, starting with a wide grid taking into account the useful part and marking the trees; an evaluation phase over the following years, where the best actual trees will be selected and finally the collection on a tighter grid of the most promising groups.
In a case of forest species collection, Zobel (1970) recommends the joining of seeds from 5 - 25 trees to form a sample. However, there is the danger of mixing different species as in the case of vaguely defined families (*Pinaceae* and *Sapotaceae*, for example).

b) Cultivated Species
Due to the clonal reproduction of many fruit trees, very often it is enough to collect only one vegetative sample of each type or variety. When the species is reproduced through seed, Hawkes (1980) recommends that one considers each human settlement as a collecting unit, as the family gardens sometimes include more than one or two trees.
Propagation of material will be easier when it can be vegetated and propagated through cuttings, as is the case for some temperate climate fruit trees.

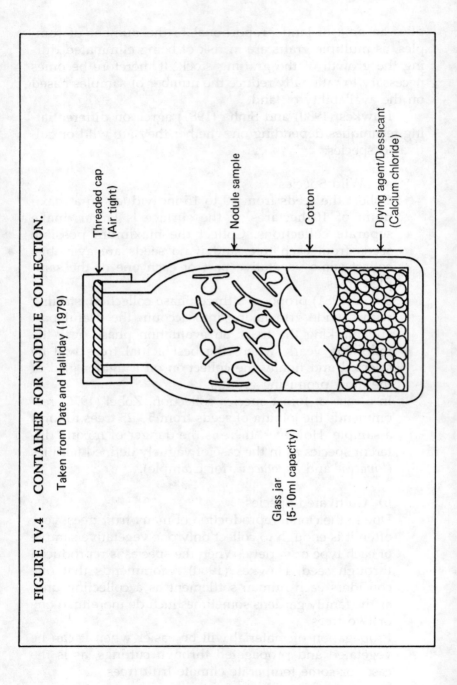

FIGURE IV.4 · CONTAINER FOR NODULE COLLECTION.
Taken from Date and Halliday (1979)

4.2.4.   *Rhizobium* nodules and pests

The collection of a legume would not be complete if it did not include the *Rhizobium* nodules associated with it.

Date and Haliday (1979) recommend the choosing of a series of typical and well-developed plants. From each of these, at least 10 nodules should be collected, which should be in good state (being rosy or white in colour at the time of cutting). Only whole nodules should be collected, cutting the side roots to avoid damage. Storage up to 14 days can be done in an easily constructed container (Figure IV.4).

In the case of diseases and pests, Sonoda (1979) recommends mainly the collection of information on observed symptoms and the capture of insects through nets and their preservation for future identification. In the case of bacteria, one can cut a piece of damaged tissue and put it into a test-tube with 1 cubic centimetre of distilled water. The macerated tissue should be later put in a growth medium. For fungi, the samples are taken with adhesive tape, which are then glued on to a microscope slide which is first moistened with a drop of lactophenol.

Ears of traditional corn selected for collection and storage.

V
Management of Information and Materials

ONCE THE COLLECTIONS have been made, material and information arrive at the genebank, where only an orderly procedure will allow for the maximum use of information and the adequate processing of the material for its future storage.

We will look at the description of the flow of material initially and then at the flow of information, for ease of explanation. In practice however, both processes take place simultaneously. Figure V.1, which describes the flow of data and material in a theoretical bank, and which is used with adaptations in various gene banks, will serve as a guideline throughout the chapter.

1. DESCRIPTION OF THE FLOW OF MATERIAL

We will look at general techniques for the management of seeds, as most seeds can be managed in a similar manner. Once the samples come in, be it from collecting or introductions, one must define if they should get into the laboratory or be planted. A decision must be taken immediately, as the survival of the vegetative material will depend on it. Waiting a weekend to plant vegetative material can cause the loss of this material. The management of vegetative reproduced species will be looked at in more detail in the next chapter.

The management of seeds of genetic resources has a certain similarity with the processing of seeds in the industry, the main difference being the small size of the

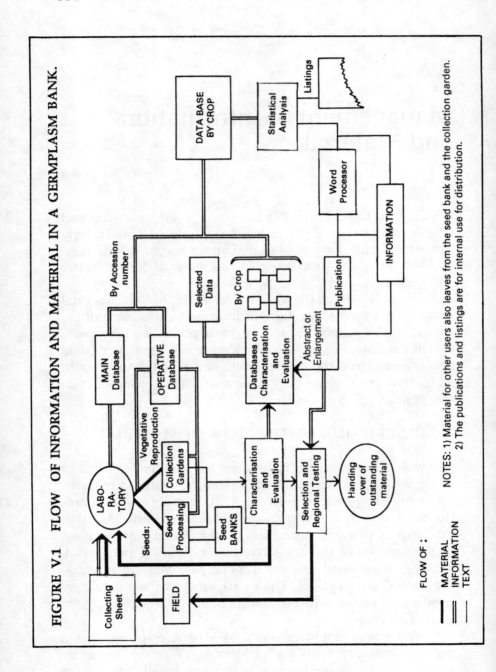

FIGURE V.1   FLOW OF INFORMATION AND MATERIAL IN A GERMPLASM BANK.

FLOW OF :

MATERIAL
INFORMATION
TEXT

NOTES: 1) Material for other users also leaves from the seed bank and the collection garden.
2) The publications and listings are for internal use for distribution.

samples and the wide range of species worked with in the case of genetic resources. When there are similarities, the explanation has been reduced as much as possible, giving more emphasis to those areas in which marked differences exist with large scale techniques.

1.1 Observation

When the material arrives at the genebank, it is necessary to observe whether the sample contains live insects and if the humidity content is high. Frequently the samples are processed only in the following days, thus they should be immediately dried to a level which will avoid germination and the development of fungi (10-15% humidity). After drying, only the samples with visible live insects will be fumigated. The presence of inert material, seeds of other species (mainly weeds), visible physical damage (broken seeds) and the possible pre-germination of some of the seeds will be determined.

The information which is obtained in this phase is coded and this allows the establishment of the processing needs.

1.2 Processing

It is important to clean the sample to ensure that only seeds of the accession will be stored. If seeds of weeds are not eliminated, the risks exist that during exchange, weeds from other zones or countries will be introduced to areas where they did not pre-exist. On the other hand, in the collection of traditional varieties, it is frequent that there will be a large mixture of phenotypes. These mixtures will be maintained as they are as they arrive to preserve the original identity of the material. It will be a decision of the user to decide whether he wants to divide the samples that he receives from the bank, according to his needs.

The cleaning can be done with laboratory cribs, which makes it easier to separate small seeds and inert material. Laboratory equipment exists for the separation of seeds through gravity, texture of the seed cover, resistance to the flow of air current, shape, colour and specific weight. These machines are generally not useful for genetic resources, as the size of the samples is small and they are more efficient for semi-industrial separation. If they are used, care should be taken to clean them very well between samples. If one is working with larger seed volumes, it is possible to look at the description of different equipment in the article by Boyd and Cabrera (1978) and in the different literature on seeds.

1.2.1 Drying

All that will be mentioned in this section on drying refers to the group of "orthodox seeds", which are defined by Roberts (1973) as: "Seeds for which the viability period increases in a logarithmic manner as one reduces the storage temperature and the moisture contents of the same". The second group are "recalcitrant seeds", which do not follow the rules which apply to most of the species and lose viability quickly, especially when dried or stored at low temperatures. The main recalcitrants species are shown in Table V.1. For these species, other storage techniques have to be used.

The most important phase of processing is the drying of seeds. The seed is a living organism and therefore susceptible to death at high temperatures. Good drying will ensure the survival of seeds for a long period of time under adequate storage conditions, whereas insufficient or excessive drying causes serious damage.

Thompson (1979) defines three "categories" of water within seed:

a) Water directly linked with seed organs, specifically inside the cell walls or as protoplasmic liquid.

b) Water linked to the seed through electromagnetic forces, as part of the structure of the seed.

c) "Free" water which is found in the cellular interstices and which can be easily withdrawn.

Table V.1 Some species with recalcitrant seeds

Araucaria spp.	Araucaria
Castanea spp.	Chestnut
Chrysophyllum cainito	Caimito
Cinnamomum ceylanicum	Cinnamon
Cocos nucifera	Coconut
Diospyros spp.	Ebony
Durio spp.	Durian
Erythroxylum coca	Coca
Garcinia spp.	Mangosteen
Hevea brasiliensis	Rubber tree
Mangifera spp.	Mango
Manilkara achras	*Zapote
Myristica fragrans	Nutmeg
Nephelium lappaceum	Rambutan
Persea spp.	Avocado
Quercus spp.	Oak
Spondias spp.	*Jocote
Swietenia mahagoni	Mahogony
Syzgium aromaticum	Colves
Thea sinensis	Tea
Theobroma cacao	Cocoa

Taken from Cromarty *et al.* (1985)

* no translation available

It is with this "free" water that we must work on during drying. Drying itself, according to Boyd (1978), takes place in two phases:

First phase, external to the seed: evaporation of moisture which is to be found on the surface of the seed, which becomes a gas in the external environment (generally air) and the extraction of that moisture through the introduction of dry air.

Second phase, internal to the seed: loss of moisture which is on the external areas of the seed and flow of moisture from the inside of the seed towards the surface.

When drying takes place quickly, seeds which are in physiological activity can be damaged. Maximum drying temperature is 45 °C, because at 52 °C almost all seeds will be killed. When drying is very slow, the risk of micro-organism growth arises as the medium temperature makes the seed batch an ideal growth medium (for the development of these).

Delouche (1980) proposes a series of basic rules for the storage of seeds, many of which are related to moisture. These rules are:

   a)   The moisture content and the temperature are the main factors influencing storage.

   b)   The moisture content of the seeds is a function of relative humidity and, to a lesser degree, of temperature.

   c)   For every 1% reduction in the moisture content of the seeds, one almost doubles their storage potential.

   d)   For each 5.6 °C reduction in the storage temperature, the seeds' storage potential is almost doubled.

   e)   Damaged, immature and broken seeds will not preserve as well as whole, mature and healthy ones.

   f)   For storage in sealed containers, the moisture content should be 2-3% lower than the one used for conventional storage.

   g)   The longevity of seed is a characteristic of the species.

The above is an example of the fact that drying is the factor which has the most influence on the survival of seeds during storage.

The development of fungi and bacteria starts when the moisture content of the seeds is higher than 13.5% and the temperature higher than 27 °C. Below these levels of moisture and temperature, no pathogens will develop. However, very often in a sample with up to 14% or 15% moisture no fungi will develop unless a very large amount of spores are to be found in the environment.

The moisture content of the seed depends on relative humidity. Relative humidity depends on the amount of water in the air and on the temperature. Air contains a certain quantity of water in the vapour state, reaching saturation point (100% relative humidity) when this vapour condenses into fog. Under normal conditions, air is below this saturation point, and there is a marked difference in the amount of water by air volume as a function of its temperature. Air at high temperatures is capable of retaining a higher amount of water, and the lower the temperature, less water will be retained in the air by per unit of volume.

To determine relative humidity, frequently expensive and sophisticated equipment is used, even though it is possible to build a simple psychrometer with two thermometers fixed side by side on a little wooden piece and which should then be moved like a rattle. One thermometer is called the dry bulb as opposed to the second one which has the mercury bulb covered with a piece of gauze which is wetted with distilled water (humid bulb). When the "rattle" is moved, the two thermometers will measure different temperatures, as the humid bulb will get colder due to the evaporation of water. If the air is saturated, no water will evaporate, and the temperature on both bulbs will be equal. The lower the relative humidity of the air, the more water will evaporate from the humid bulb and therefore the temperature of that thermometer will be lower than for the dry bulb.

This relation is presented in the psychrometric table (Figure V.2) which allow us to know the relative humidity as a function of the temperature of the dry and wet bulbs. This same table allows us to calculate the relative humidity of air after heating it up.

For example, if the temperature measured is 23°C for the humid bulb and 27°C for the dry bulb, we would look up the psychrometric table and read that the relative humidity is 70%. As we heat the air up to 35°C, we would finally have air with an approximate relative humidity of 44%, adequate to dry seeds. Other examples and uses of the psychometric table can be found in the article by Cromarty (1984).

The equilibrium moisture content is the content of moisture which the seed has once it balances with the air moisture. At this point the seed will neither absorb nor lib-

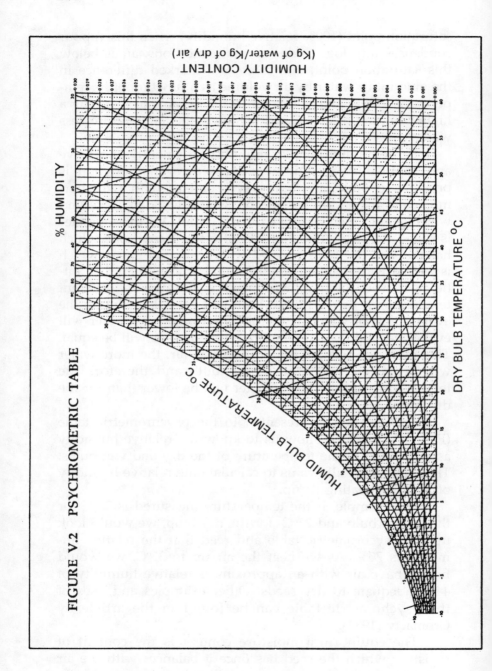

FIGURE V.2 PSYCHROMETRIC TABLE

erate moisture as long as the relative humidity or the temperature does not change.

The equilibrium moisture is characteristic for each species. In the following figures, one can look at the equilibrium moisture content of sorghum (Figure V.3) and maize (Figure V.4) as a function of relative humidity and temperature. This phenomenon is almost identical for most species, and its equilibrium moisture contents is reached in a period ranging from a few days up to two or three months (Justice and Bass, 1978).

For conventional species, the equilibrium moisture content at different relative humidities and temperatures has been reported (Table V.2). One can see that seed with high starch content will attract more water than those with high oil content. The moisture absorption capacity of cereals is therefore higher, and legumes will have a lower equilibrium moisture contents.

One of the problems of the drying of seeds of genetic resources is the small volume with which one works, and the fact that very often one is dealing with non-conventional species, about which neither the equilibrium moisture content nor the ideal moisture content for storage is known. The person in charge of the laboratory will have to decide the moisture content he wants to get to before the seeds are stored if he does not work with conventional species.

In the case of conventional species, some recommendations exist (Table V.3), for the moisture contents at which one should store seeds in sealed containers. When seed is stored in sealed containers, the seed should be dried 2% below the recommended moisture content for the storage in non-sealed containers, as the risk of water condensation increases.

Seed drying can be achieved through various techniques. The simplest one is to keep the seed under the sun in open air until it equilibrates with the relative humidity. Very often the equilibrium moisture content reached by this means is too high for long term storage of genetic resources and there is also the risk of over-heating the seeds.

The artificial drying techniques are of two types:

FIGURE V.3   EQUILIBRIUM MOISTURE CONTENT
IN SORGHUM.

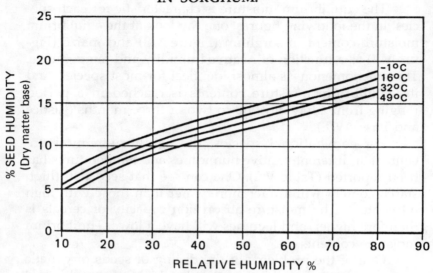

FIGURE V.4   EQUILIBRIUM MOISTURE CONTENT
IN MAIZE.

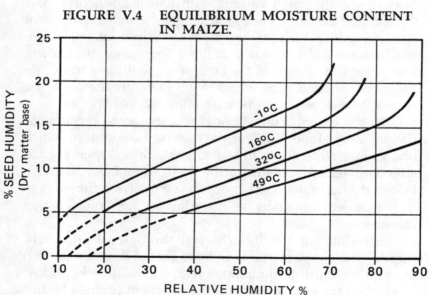

Table V.2 Equilibrium moisture of the seeds of certain species at different relative humidities at 25°C.

Species	Relative Humidity (%)					
	20	30	45	60	75	90
Alfalfa	4.5	6.4	7.4	8.6	9.3	-
Aubergine	-	6.3	8.0	9.8	11.9	-
Barley	6.0	8.4	10.0	12.1	14.4	19.5
Beans	4.8	6.8	9.4	12.0	15.0	-
Lima beans (*Phaseolus lunatus*)	-	7.7	9.2	11.0	13.8	-
Beet	4.0	5.8	7.6	9.4	11.2	-
Bermuda grass	-	8.1	9.2	10.8	13.6	17.2
Buckwheat	-	9.1	10.8	12.7	15.0	19.1
Carrot	5.9	6.8	7.9	9.2	11.6	-
Celery	7.0	7.8	9.0	10.4	12.4	-
Chili	4.5	6.0	7.8	9.2	11.0	-
Cotton	4.5	6.0	7.5	9.1	14.4	18.0
Cucumber	4.3	5.6	7.1	8.4	10.1	-
Lettuce	4.2	5.1	5.9	7.1	9.6	-
Linen	-	5.6	6.3	7.9	10.0	15.2
Maize (Corn)	-	8.4	10.5	12.9	14.8	19.0
Maize, sweet (Corn)	5.8	7.0	9.0	10.6	12.8	-
Millet (Pearl)	-	8.5	9.8	12.0	13.7	17.0
Mustard	3.2	4.6	6.3	7.8	9.4	-
Oats	-	8.0	9.6	11.8	13.8	18.5
Okra	7.2	8.3	10.0	11.2	13.1	-
Onion	6.8	8.0	9.5	11.2	13.4	-
Peanut	-	4.2	5.6	7.2	9.8	13.0
Peas	7.3	8.6	10.1	11.9	15.0	-
Radish	3.8	5.1	6.8	8.3	10.2	-
Red Clover	-	7.2	8.2	9.2	13.2	18.4
Rice	-	9.0	10.7	12.6	14.4	18.1
Rye	-	8.7	10.5	12.2	14.8	20.6
Rye grass	-	7.5	10.0	11.2	13.8	17.0
Sorghum	-	8.6	10.5	12.0	15.2	18.8
Soyabean	-	6.5	7.4	9.3	13.1	18.8
Spinach	6.5	7.8	9.5	11.1	13.2	-
Sudan grass	-	8.6	10.1	1.6	13.2	18.8
Sunflower	-	5.1	6.5	8.0	10.0	15.0
Timothy	-	-	9.5	11.4	13.6	17.2
Tomato	5.0	6.3	7.8	9.2	11.1	-
Turnip	4.0	5.1	6.3	7.4	9.0	-
Watermelon	4.8	6.1	7.6	8.8	10.4	-
Wheat (soft red)	-	8.6	10.6	11.9	14.6	19.7
White Clover	-	8.6	9.9	11.8	15.0	19.7
Winter pumpkin	4.3	5.6	7.4	9.0	10.8	·

Figures compiled from different sources by the author and by the Seed Technology Laboratory of Mississippi State University.

Table V.3 Maximum recommended humidity contents for the storage of seeds in sealed containers

Species	Humidity (%)
Alfalfa	6
Aubergines	6
Barley	10
Beans	8
Beet	7.5
Broccoli	5
Brussels sprouts	5
Cabbage	5
Carrot	7
Cauliflower	5
Celery	5.5
Cucumber	6
Flowers	6 - 7.5
Grasses	8 - 9
Lettuce	5.5
Linen	7
Maize (Corn)	10
Maize, sweet (Corn)	8
Melon	6
Mustard	5
Oats	10
Onion	6
Peas	7
Pepper	5
Pumpkin	6
Red clover	7
Rye	10
Soyabeans	8
Spinach	7
Tomato	5
Turnip	6.5
Watermelon	6
Wheat	10

Various sources.

a) Drying through the flow of hot air
b) Drying with dry air.

For drying with heated air, one should never use temperatures higher than 45°C, as this can kill the seed. It is important to remember that in the case of immature seeds, independent of the speed of drying, there will be a problem due to the low quality of the original seeds (Bass, 1975). Harrington (1970) recommends that in order to dry seeds down to 6% moisture content, one can use hot air with 15% relative humidity for two hours, starting with air at 90% humidity and 5°C heated up to 35°C whereby one arrives at 15% relative humidity. Unfortunately, in tropical climate the initial low temperature is not often to be found.

Drying techniques with dessicants are used both before and during storage. Drying agents usually used are calcium chloride, calcium oxide, magnesium chloride and magnesium sulphate. Until now, germination of seeds has only been tested after drying with calcium chloride and calcium oxide, which reduces the relative humidity down to 30% and 10% respectively (Nakamura, cited by Bass, 1975). There is also a contradictory report from Kondo and Isshiki (1936, cited by Justice and Bass, 1978) in which they mention that it was necessary to use 1 kg of calcium chloride or 3 kg of calcium oxide to reduce by 1% the moisture content of 1.8 bushels of rice seeds.

The most common highly hygroscopic (moisture-sensitive, water attracting) compound used for seed drying is silica gel (CIAT, personal communication; Roland Loiselle, personal communication). Industry reports a 27% absorption by weight of silica at 80% relative humidity. In practice, one does not work at such high relative humidities and real absorption, as one dries maize seeds from 12% to 9%, is therefore only 15% by weight of silica.

The size of samples being small, one cannot determine the moisture content with the two conventional techniques. The technique of drying with an oven destroys part of the sample, which is not justified due to the small original size of the accessions. The moisture determination through electric conductivity works only with samples of 100 grams or more. These amounts of seeds are rare in genetic resources work with small seeded species and there is also a 1% or higher error in known species, due to differences in oil content. This error is much larger in species whose conductivity is not known and variability is larger than in modern varieties.

Thompson (1979) proposes a method to determine moisture contents in small samples, using a sealed jar with a known amount of seeds. With the sample, a piece of paper with lithium compounds is introduced. The equilibrium moisture content of air will be a function of the amount of water liberated by the seed, and the colouring of the paper will depend on relative humidity. Making a parallel extrapolation with similar species, one can estimate the moisture content of the seed. Unfortunately, this kind of paper is not readily available.

An empirical and efficient method is to determine the moisture content with a reference sample which is generally commercial seeds and to extrapolate the equilibrium moisture content to other samples of the same species.

The technique utilised to determine moisture content in seed production is not recommended for work on genetic resources as it is destructive, even though it is recommended by the IBPGR (Ellis *et al.*, 1985). Seeds, frequently ground, are introduced in an oven at constant temperature of 101-105° C for 15-17 hours in the case of seed with high oil content and at 130-133° C for 1-4 hours in the case of seeds with low oil content (Hanson, 1985). The difference between the initial weight and the final weight is due to the evaporation of seed moisture. The moisture content is calculated based on the total weight according to the following equation:

$$\% \text{ Moisture content} = \frac{\text{Weight of water (g)}}{\text{Total weight (g)}} \times 100$$

Where total weight is the sum of weight of water plus dry matter.

1.2.2 Fumigation

If the seed does not show insect infestation and is stored at temperatures below 0°C, fumigation is superfluous as the cold will not allow the development of insects. Once the seed is dried and if storage is to be at temperatures above 0°C, it should be treated with some product which will kill the insects in the sample. Aluminium phosphide (commercial name Phostoxin) kills the insects, without any reported damage to the germination of seeds and without leaving residues of the fumigation process. It is recommended to use from 0.75 to 1.5 gram of Phosphine per cubic metre. With a tablet of 0.6 gram one can obtain approximately 0.3 gram of Phosphine, the maximum recommended dose for a 200 litre drum. Phosphine is a potent poison to man. The maximum permitted concentration is 0.18 to 0.54 milligrams per cubic metre (Monro, 1970).

Fumigation itself is done using 200 litre drums in which the open flasks or trays are introduced with the material to fumigate within them. The drums have a sealed cover (for example paint drums). To fumigate one should use plastic gloves. The tablets are deposited in a container in order to keep the ashes which form after the reaction of the tablets with air moisture from falling into the samples. Once the drum is closed it is labelled and kept close for 7-10 days so that the insects hatch and the gas kills them, as this gas is not effective against the eggs. The cylinder must be opened in an aired place to avoid poisoning of those who handle the drums. Material is stored immediately to avoid re-infection with pathogens.

1.3 Germination and viability tests

Before storing seeds, it is necessary to make a germination test to ensure that one is storing living seeds and not dead grains.

The germination test is a process which is done in the laboratory and during which the seeds are put under optimum germination conditions, in order to measure the passage from a latent or low physiological activities stage to a stage of vegetative growth. Sometimes the seed may be alive, but will not germinate. In the case of species with dormancy, viability tests should be made.

During the germination test the seed must have water and an adequate environment for its development, including an adequate temperature, and in certain cases chemical products and other factors.

For each species, the ideal conditions for its germination are a combination of the aforementioned factors. Rules on the ideal germination conditions for seeds of many conventional species have been reported (ISTA, 1966; AOSA, 1981) and even for some lesser known species (Ellis *et al.*, 1985b). For non-conventional species it will be necessary to make a choice to determine those conditions. We will now look in detail at the conditions needed for germination.

The presence of distilled water is achieved through a humid environment. The seed generally will not germinate when it is totally covered with water, as it has no oxygen

Table V.4: Temperature ranges in which seeds of different species germinate.

Species	Temperature (°C)		
	Minimum	Optimum	Maximum
Zea mays	8-10	32-35	40-44
Oryza sativa	10-12	30-37	40-42
Triticum aestivum	3-5	15-31	30-43
Hordeum sativum	3-5	19-27	30-40
Secale cereale	3-5	25-31	30-40
Avena sativa	3-5	25-31	30-40
Cucumis melo	16-19	30-40	45-50
Solanum carolinense	20	20-35	35-40
Nicotiana tabacum	10	24	30
Glycine max	8	32	40

Source: Mayer and Poljakoff (1963)

to breathe (Thompson, 1979). Generally, the moisture is achieved through an absorbent medium like paper towels or sand. The most commonly used substrates are: seeds on blotter paper, blotter paper with the seeds in the centre (2 to 4 sheets), sand, vermiculite and soil. The differences in the substrate used are for practical reasons. It is recommended that sand or some voluminous medium be used in the case of seeds whose size would not allow the contact of the whole surface with water if paper was used.

Most seeds germinate at a temperature between 15 and 35°C even though with a temperature of 20°C good results can be obtained. Mayer and Poljakoff (1963) compiled a table with the temperature ranges at which some species germinate (Table V.4). The optimum temperature is different according to the physical state of the seed and the date at which the counting of the germinated seeds is made. Cooper and Quayle (1968) reported differences in the vigour of four varieties of clover according to the temperature at which the germination test was made. So we can assume that the optimum temperatures will be different not only between species, but even between varieties. In certain cases it is necessary to use alternating temperatures to break dormancy. Thompson (1979) reported that in grasses, dormancy is so common that a fluctuating regime of 20°C for 16 hours and 30°C for 8 hours is used, which reproduces the fluctuation between day and night.

Light is also used to break dormancy in the case of grasses, and it also avoids the elongation of the plants due to darkness. However, white, red and green light can inhibit the germination in certain cases, for example in *Dioscorea* (Okagami and Kawai, 1977).

There are some chemical substances which have an effect in inducing germination. Mayer and Poljakoff (1963) reported the use of potassium nitrate, ethylene, giberellic acid and quinetine. All those substances replace, in certain cases, light for the breaking of dormancy. Potassium nitrate is the most commonly used product among this group. The ISTA (1986) recommends the use of potassium nitrate in concentration of 0.2% in the germination tests of seeds of many grasses. Some of these products also break dormancy, as is the case of giberellic acid, used in lettuce and potatoes.

1.3.1 Dormancy

Dormancy is a phenomenon during which no germination occurs even when the seed is under optimum conditions for its germination. Before genetic resources are stored one should be sure if the material is dead or dormant, as otherwise there will be an increase in the number of reported live seeds as a function of the storage time, with all the confusions this implies.

There are different types of dormancy. Each one can be de-activated in one way or another. For practical reasons, in certain cases one does not try to break dormancy but to just make a viability test. We will look now at the dormancy types and later at the viability tests.

a) *Dormancy due to immature seed*
This kind of dormancy occurs when the seed has just been harvested and needs a post-ripening phase before germinating. It is the protection mechanism through which most of the plant species protect themselves in order not to germinate when it rains whilst on the mother plant.
b) *Dormancy due to mechanical resistance of the seed cover*
This dormancy is not very important, unless the plant is not very vigorous. Internally the germination process starts, but plants cannot develop as they cannot break the cover, as is the case in sunflower and mango.
c) *Impermeable seed cover ("hard seed")*
This dormancy occurs due to the impermeability of the seed cover (testa) to gases as well as to liquids. When the seed cover is broken or perforated, germination begins immediately. For the breaking of this type of dormancy, it is necessary to break the testa through mechanical scarification (sand-paper the seed) or with

acid treatments, as in the case of the genus *Brassica*.
d) *Biochemical dormancy of the embryo.*
Germination does not occur due to the presence of germination inhibitors. These inhibitors are the same inhibitors which can be found in other parts of the plant, basically abcissic and phenolic compounds (cafeic acid, cumaric acid, pirogalol, resorcinol, catecol). The inhibitions through these compounds can be de-activated with the use of giberellines (Andrews and Burrows, 1972; Bewley, 1979), for example in the case of citrus trees and cucurbits, by physical means like stratification, and with the use of various types of energy. The last two methods have been studied in the review by Heydecker and Coolbear (1970). It is important not to forget that high concentration of giberellic acid may also be inhibiting (Mayer and Poljakoff, 1963).

1.3.2. Viability Tests

When, for practical reasons one decides not to break dormancy, tests are made through which one can determine the viability of the seed. Viability is understood as the capacity of the seed to germinate once the factor which causes dormancy has been withdrawn.

The most commonly used test to determine viability is the **tetrazolium test**. This test determines which organs of the seed are alive and which show high physiological activity. Tetrazolium salt (2,3,5-triphenyl tetrazolium) at the commonly used concentrations (0.1 to 1%) reacts with the hydrogen produced by the respiration processes of the seed, producing a red staining.

The procedure for the tetrazolium tests are described in the manuals by Grabe (1970) and Moreno (1976). The result of the test is a red or rosy pink staining of the embryos of live seeds which are dormant. A stronger colouring in certain cases does not necessarily imply healthy physiological activity. No colouring in some cases means that the solution did not penetrate the seed but it generally means that the seed or part of it is dead.

1.4 Packaging

When the germination test has shown that there is enough live seed, the last phase of processing in a laboratory takes place: packaging.

For the storage of genetic resources, it is necessary to keep the seed dry. The high energy consumption and therefore costs to maintain large spaces at low temperatures and simultaneously at low relative humidity continuously make it more efficient to keep the seed in sealed containers in order not to have to worry about the relative humidity of the storeroom.

The techniques used for storage have been large coldrooms in which seeds are stored in glass jars sealed with wax (in the Nordic gene banks) or in sealed metal cans (in the International Rice Research Institute, CENARGEN – National Genetic Resources Centre – in Brazil and other genebanks). Presently, the development of polylaminated materials allows the utilisation of envelopes, which is more efficient in space use and therefore allows the storage of more samples with less refrigeration cost.

Experiments done by Bass (1973) and Clark and Bass (1975), in which the permeability to water of six different laminated materials was studied, demonstrated that many of the materials are not fully water-proof. The comparison of the packaging materials, most of which were polylaminated, showed that it is necessary to have a sheet of aluminium of at least 0.00035 millimetres thick to avoid the flow of moisture from the outside. Envelopes made with much thicker coats of polyester and acetate and Milar, did not stop the flow of moisture over a 2 or 3 year period, under storage conditions of 10°C and 70% relative humidity. Even though the real storage conditions are at lower relative humidity and lower temperatures, this test during a limited number of years enables one to extrapolate the potential resistance of the materials to the flow of moisture. The same papers mentioned show that certain polylaminated material gets damaged at low temperatures and high moisture levels, and the paper on the outside layer disintegrates. In certain cases the material was good for storage but there was a problem due to the inadequate sealing of the containers.

For the sealing of the containers, Justice and Bass (1978) recommend the use of temperatures from 140 to 200°C, for approximately 3 seconds with a pressure of 3 kg/cm2. These recommendations are not applicable when a hand sealing machine is used in which one does not control the pressure or the temperature. In this case it is necessary to have quality control after the sealing, and for safety, a double-sealing process is done.

Another factor which has been studied as related to packaging is the type of atmosphere to be used. Bass *et al.* (1963), Bass (1978) and Bass and Stanwood (1978) stored sorghum, sesame, safflower and clover in air, in vacuum and in some gases (nitrogen, carbon dioxide, helium and argon). In the case of safflower and sesame, temperature and moisture were the main factors determining the evolution of the seed's germination during storage. There were no differences in the atmosphere used for storage. In the case of sorghum, the most important factor was temperature and there was also no effect due to the type of gas used in the sealed container. In the case of clover, there was no improvement in the survival of seeds after 8 and 16 years of storage using other gases instead of air. In this case, the moisture content was also the main factor for the deterioration of seeds, having temperature as a second factor.

An interesting result of the series of tests, on top of demonstrating the uselessness of special gases for storage, is that in the case of seed storage with high moisture contents, it was more efficient to store them in paper bags than in sealed envelopes, as the seed dried quickly at low temperatures. The paper envelopes used as a control in the case of clover were almost as good as sealed cans.

Depending on the type of material with which one works, the seed is stored either in only one container or in samples of approximately 100 seeds in separated ones. The advantage of separate containers (envelopes) with 100 seeds is that it allows to have material available for distribution as well as for germination test and regeneration activities.

The idea of using dehydrating material such as silica gel within the sealed containers has been put forward. This has been reported by various authors (cited by Justice and Bass, 1978) and has good results. The costs however can be higher and one should evaluate the validity of, and need for, this procedure.

2. DESCRIPTION OF THE INFORMATION FLOW

Work with genetic resources is associated to the management of large volumes of information. This is due to the large number of samples with which a genebank generally works, as well as to the information associated to the samples (passport information, physical location, movement of samples, viability, characterisation and evaluation).

Finlay and Konzak (1970) mentioned the need to create a computer system, which would be compatible for all those who work on genetic resources, in order to centralise and distribute the information of researchers at a global level. That way, the exchange of information and material would be faster and more efficient as all systems would have compatible information.

Based on this idea, the IBPGR established in 1974 an agreement with the University of Colorado for the creation of a germplasm information management system (IBPGR, 1975). After four years of work and one and a half million dollars paid to the University of Colorado (IBPGR, 1978), the report of IBPGR for 1980 (IBPGR, 1981) says: "From 1975 to 1979 the largest part of IBPGR's work on the information problem was executed by a team in the University of Colorado. During this period, the team promoted amongst collectors and breeders the consciousness of the need for information management. Their contract expired in 1979 and presently their information area will be directly managed by IBPGR". This means that EXIR, the computer package which was elaborated for the international management of genetic resources, ceased from being used and did not get the adequate maintenance for its functioning. Presently, it is not being used at an international level, but most of the personnel of this project ended up working for the United States Department of Agriculture, using the previous investment to develop the genetic resources information system (GRIN) which the United States Department of Agriculture presently uses.

Working with computers, data management has various specific characteristics. It is necessary to consider that the reading and storing of information are done in a different way from the traditonal one, in files or cardholders. It is necessary to use a procedure to standardise the data transformation, codifying and transcription so that it can be then used in computers.

When data is taken in some of the work phases of genetic resources, it is ideal to write them down in such a way that it will be possible to transfer them directly into the computer, without having to copy them again to coding sheets, as after each copy new mistakes are introduced. The most precise information would be the one which got into the computer with fewer intermediate copying stages. First, one must know beforehand which data will be taken and how much space it uses. Each letter, number, symbol or empty space will use one space (1 byte in a computer). Then, one elaborates a data sheet which will delimit the available space for each data item, making it clear to the user that this space corresponds to a certain number of bytes and that it doesn't make sense to write with smaller letters in order to cram more information in the boxes but to limit the number of characters to the number of boxes in the sheet. The collecting sheet is one format of this kind. In the following lines we will see other formats of similar use. Shafton (1979) describes the methods for the preparation of germplasm data bases, but his proposals are presently partially obsolete due to the use of microcomputers which allows for more flexibility at work.

The description which follows is related to a genetic resources management package which is used in REGEN in

Nicaragua and INIPA in Peru (Figure V.1).

As the collecting sheet comes from the field the validity and clarity of data is reviewed. Some keys which the collector may not know are codified. When the collecting sheet (as well as the genetic material!) has been verified and is found to be in adequate condition, an accession number is assigned to the collection. Information is introduced to the passport data base and provisional listings are given to the people in charge of processsing the material in the fields and in the laboratory.

In the laboratory, the necessary tests are made and the cleaning and pre-treatment of material for its storage are executed. During this process, the following management data is taken:

1. Accession number.
2. Material in the field or in laboratory.
3. Collecting sheet number.
4. Date of introduction to the laboratory or field.
5. Weight in grams or number of plants if the material is in the field.
6. Percent of seeds with insect damage.
7. Percent of pre-germinated seeds.
8. Date of the germination test.
9. Percent germination in this first test.
10. Date of the second germination test.
11. Percent germination in the second germination test.
12. Date of the third germination test.
13. Percent germination in the third germination test.
14. Physical location of the material.
15. Number or type of containers.

The data 1 to 9, 14 and 15 are taken during the first phase of the laboratory work and are written directly on a coding sheet (Figure V.5). Based on the typical weight of 100 seeds of each species, stored in the computer, the number of seeds is calculated using the information on weight of sample.

As in many cases, species for which environmental conditions or the adequate temperatures for their germina-

FIGURE V.5 CODIFICATION SHEET FOR LABORATORY DATA.

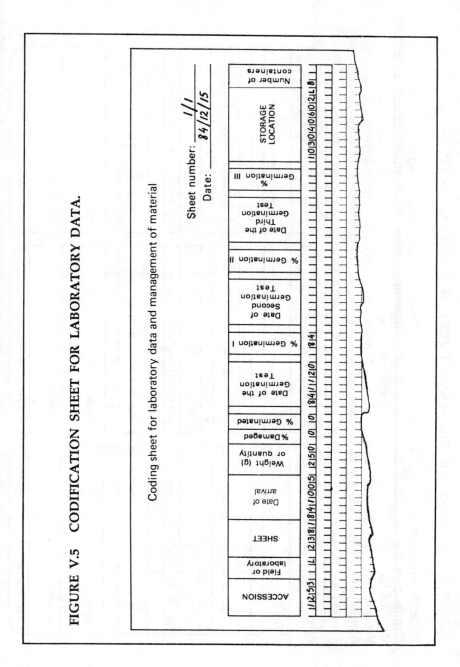

Coding sheet for laboratory data and management of material

Sheet number: _____ / / / _____

Date: _____ 84/12/15 _____

FIGURE V.6 FORMAT FOR THE MANAGEMENT OF GERMINATION TESTS.

Accession number .... Control .... Sheet number .... Page .... of.............
Common name .... Scientific name ....
Date of harvest ....Reception date .... Notes ....
Weight ....100 seed weight .... Number of seeds .... % Humidity ....
Maximum number of seeds to be used .... Presence of insects ....

A

— Replications — Seeds — °C —

DATE

Rep.	DAY				
1					
2					
3					
4					
5					
Total					
Days	Healthy	Fungi	Bacteria	Empty	

NOTES:

SUBSTRATE:

% GERMINATION

B

— Replications — Seeds — °C —

DATE

Rep.	DAY				
1					
2					
3					
4					
5					
Total					
Days	Healthy	Fungi	Bacteria	Empty	

NOTES:

SUBSTRATE:

% GERMINATION

C

— Replications — Seeds — °C —

DATE

Rep.	DAY				
1					
2					
3					
4					
5					
Total					
Days	Healthy	Fungi	Bacteria	Empty	

NOTES:

SUBSTRATE:

% GERMINATION

tion are unknown have to be tested, a sheet is used (Figure V.6) in which a control is kept on the changes in the environment, temperature and other conditions, during the germination tests. That way one has a register of the optimum conditions for future germination tests of that species and also a clinical sheet of the evolution and problems of each one of the accessions.

Based on the results of the germination tests, it is determined if the material can be stored directly in the coldroom. If the result of the germination test is above 60%, it is considered as material which can enter storage. If it is less than 60% and it is a species that generally has high germination percentages, it is necessary to plant the seed for its re-generation.

The physical location key of the material in storage is generated based on the specific position inside the coldroom with numbered shelves. Taking as an example the key of materials stored in a cold-room shown in Figure V.7:

1   03   04   06   02   LB

This number would mean that the material is stored in cold-room number 1, on the third shelf, at the fourth level, at the sixth row, in the second column or position, in a large bottle.

The alternatives for the last two letters are:

LB = large bottle (1 litre)
MB = medium bottle (0.5 litre)
SB = small bottle (100 cm³)
LE = large envelope
ME = medium envelope
SE = small envelope

If the material has been handed out for field planting, the data sheet described in Figure V.5 is completed with data items 1 to 5 and the physical location key. In the case of material kept in the fields, the location key is different. There are two main types of collection gardens.

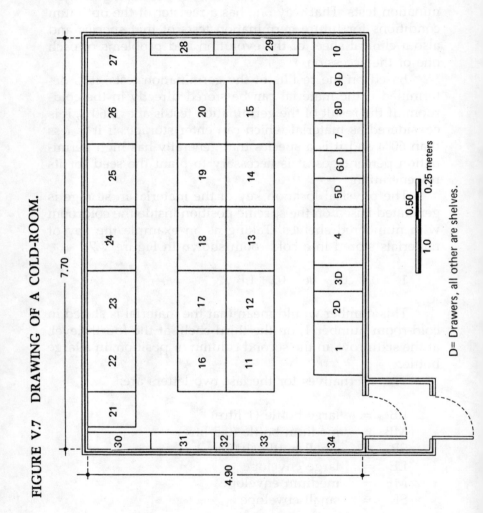

FIGURE V.7   DRAWING OF A COLD-ROOM.

D= Drawers, all other are shelves.

Those which are stored as a unit surface (for example parcels of 3 x 2 metres in the case of pasture) and those which are stored with a certain number of individual plants (fruit trees, trees in general).

The organisation principle is the physical location of each parcel or plant based on orthogonal (square) coordinates. The starting point is always located at the furthermost South and West corners in the collection garden. This is done in order to ensure that, even if the map got lost one would be able to find the location of each accession based on the coordinates stored in the computer, as the starting point is known.

The definitions used are:

First digit: experimental station or field or area.

Second and third digits: type of collection gardens (citrus, mango, pasture, etc.)

Fourth and fifth digits: number of plots or plants in the South-North direction, starting with the plots located in the furthermost South corner.

Seventh and eighth digits: number of plots or plants in the West-East direction, starting with the plots located in the furtermost West corner.

An example is shown in Figure V.8, which correspond to a chayote (*Sechium edule*) collection in Mexico. The accession 232 with collecting sheet 2201 is in the position 0608, which means that it is in the sixth position from South to North and the eighth position from West to East.

The coded information is introduced to the data base on management of material. A listing is generated for the management of the accessions and labels are printed with the basic information of the stored accessions. These labels are glued on the containers which have been in provisional storage generally in a drying room, to reduce their mois-

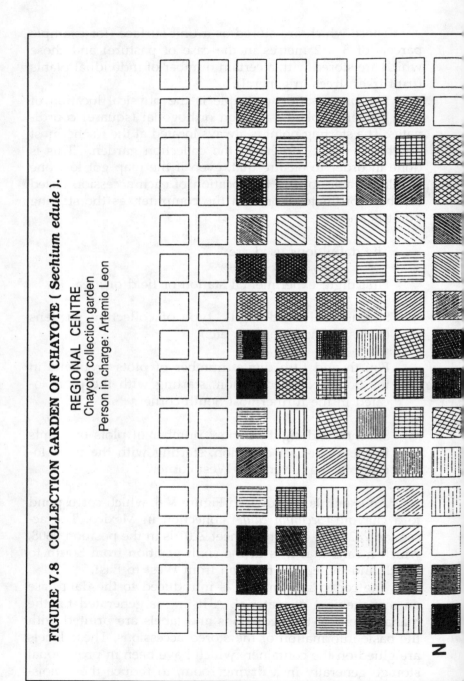

FIGURE V.8 COLLECTION GARDEN OF CHAYOTE (*Sechium edule*).

REGIONAL CENTRE
Chayote collection garden
Person in charge: Artemio Leon

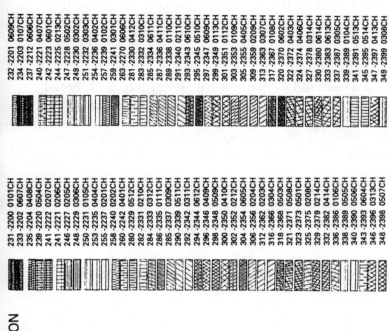

LEGEND: ACCESSION

Key to the legend: Accession-sheet, south-north, west-east, quantity

ture contents. Once labelled, the material is introduced into
the cold-room.

At this point all the information should already be in
the data base. The consistency of the information in the
computer is verified against the written documents (collecting sheet, laboratory data, etc.), the typing mistakes are cor-
rected and a general listing for the security file as well as
two reduced management listing are printed, the first one
with the accessions stored in the cold-room, the second one
for the accessions in the field, for the person responsible for
each one of the areas.

When a demand is made for material which is stored
in the genebank and if sufficient material is there, a list of
the material which can be delivered is printed. If not enough
material is available for exchange, a listing establishes which
accessions should be multiplied whenever the planting sea-
sons comes.

Forage collection garden in Huatuzco, Veracruz, Mexico.

VI
Conservation, Storage and Regeneration

THE BIOLOGICALLY SOUNDEST WAY to preserve genetic resources is to keep them in the environment in which they develop. This can be done when the environment is balanced and there are few possibilities that it will be thrown off-balance. *In situ* (on-site) conservation is that which exists naturally. The other way to preserve genetic resources is in collections, be it in the shape of collecting gardens or seedbanks, pollen, tissues, cells or genes in stores.

1. *IN SITU* CONSERVATION

In theory, the conservation of plants *in situ* allows the preservation of cultivated and wild species without the need for big expenditures, based on the political decisions taken by the authorities of the country and the area to be conserved. It is essential to remember that the first and main actors of such a proposal will be the people who live in the area. Some conservationists, mainly in the North, consider that nature as a whole is more important than man's daily survival in the South. In the case of wild species, this means ecological reservations which generally need to cover vast areas, as the species are rarely found in monoculture conditions or even at high densities. These ecological reserves have problems in developing countries, striving to balance economic, administrative and practical factors, with the need for conservation. *In situ* storage, even though good in theory, is realistic only when it is acceptable to the people, not in conflict with national priorities and when the state can ensure its continuity.

Montes (1978) proposed that the conservation of genetic resources in Mexico should be accepted as a national priority, with the support of governmental institutions. The measures for the creation of *in situ* conservation and basic research on the mechanisms to be used have not been worked on very much, even though in Mexico, as in the rest of Latin America, certain areas exist which should become genetic resource reservations. The Lacandone jungle has been decreed a "biosphere reserve", with a surface area of 1,200,000 ha, but it is simultaneously one of the country's agricultural frontiers and an oil extracting area. Therefore, its stability can hardly be ensured. There are a few national parks which can maintain relative ecological stability. Unfortunately, most of these are found in transition and pine areas, above 2,500 metres, and for that reason genetic variability of the humid tropics is not represented.

In situ conservation of fruit trees and plants used in peasant's gardens is not only feasible, but it allows a better genetic resources programmes and maintains the control of germplasm in the hands of the people who created it. In Nicaragua, outstanding trees are selected in the family gardens, and the owner is asked to take care of that plant specially, as it is part of the patrimony of the country. The peasant becomes therefore a participant of modern research process and preserves the tree, knowing that his work is being recognised.

In the case of annually cultivated species, *in situ* storage is more difficult as one must constantly control the environment where the material is kept, and take care that no new species or varieties are introduced. Rural reality in the Third World makes this difficult as traditional production is changing through the introduction of modern-bred varieties to traditional farm plots. To propose the conservation of traditional varieties without significantly breeding and selecting them means to force the peasants to maintain low levels of productivity and to deny them the advantages of some of the advances of modern agronomy.

A solution proposed by Kuckuck (1968, cited by

Frankel, 1970) is to create small areas of a half to 1 ha. in which traditional varieties would be cultivated under the control of agricultural engineers. These areas would change due to the influence of environment and would maintain their heterogeneity, even though it is improbable that they would maintain their original composition, considering the bias of the professional training of the agronomists.

2.   STORAGE IN COLLECTION

Another method for the preservation of genetic resources is in collection gardens, where the plants are kept under normal growing conditions. On the other hand, one can also have the storage of seeds, storage through tissue culture and storage of tissues and seeds at ultra low temperatures. We will see when each one of these types of storage is best suited and the techniques to be utilised.

2.1 Collection gardens

The collection gardens (or clonal gardens) are used for asexually propagated species and for trees, especially in the case of species with recalcitrant seeds. In the case of perennials, the use of collection gardens allows the maintainance of genetic information in a stable manner, even though it is necessary to use large areas. Another advantage is that these plants will be available for multiplication and testing all through their growing periods. In the case of short lived plants, this should also be tried.

Hawkes (1970) recommends that the collections of asexually propagated species (plants which are not planted through seeds) with short life cycle be established as close as possible to the collection area of the samples, or at least close to the area where they will be used for breeding or evaluation. The planting, with some difference between species, must be done with a spacing that will prevent the vegetative parts of different plants from mingling, therefore preventing the mixing of accessions and disease transmission. One must take into account the photoperiod requirements of the plant, as without a certain photoperiod some plants will never produce reproductive organs.

As a last point, Hawkes (1970) recommends that when real seeds are produced (as in the case of cassava, sweet potato and potato), one should harvest the seed of similar plants and bulk it. He also recommends lengthening the dormancy period of tubers in order to avoid the cost problem of planting every year. In the case of potato, with an adequate treatment of the tuber, it is possible to plant it once every three years.

Thompson (1974) mentioned the possibility for a continuity from botanical gardens to seed banks. In the case of asexually propagated plants the aforementioned techniques should be used to maintain the variability of the accession and at the same time to have botanical seed for other uses.

Even though there are specific recommendations on the number of plants which should be maintained for each accession of vegetative (asexual) reproduction, theoretically one plant would be enough to maintain the variability of the clone. For safety reasons, a minimum of two plants at two places are used.

In plants which are propagated through seeds, the variability problem is a little more complex. However, it is not possible to store 300 coconut trees for each accession, taking an example of IBPGR's recommendation, as the collection gardens would not be manageable due to their size.

Two examples could help to clarify the different solutions which can be applied.

1)   Collection of chayote (*Sechium edule*) in the Huatusco Regional Centre (Huatusco, Veracruz), from the Chapingo Autonomous University in Mexico.

In this case, over a hundred accessions of chayote are managed. During characterisation, the collection was in a garden where each accession was represented by two plants planted in one place utilising 9 m^2 per plot. When characterisation was finished, the area was reduced. It was found that chayote produces a root (*chayotestle*), which sprouts again after the dry season. As the *chayotestle* with shoots can be subdivided for multiple planting, two replicates of each one of the accessions were planted in separate plots, with one metre between plants and between rows, with a systematic trimming to avoid the excessive development of the plant. When a plant was needed for exchange, either a part of the *chayotestle* is taken or the plant was self-pollinated. That way variability is maintained, there is a better security as one has two plants, and the area used is reduced from 900 m² to 200 m².

2)   Aroid collection of Mesoamerica

The CATIE (Tropical Agricultural Centre for Research and Education, Costa Rica) had the Mesoamerican aroid collection in a collection garden. A copy of that collection was handed over to the Genetic Resources programme in Nicaragua for evaluation. In Nicaragua the collection was planted at two locations with different climates, with four plants at each location (after multiplication). *Colocasia spp.* adapted itself better in the humid climate and some died in the dry climate. The opposite occurred with the *Xanthosoma spp.* As a large part of the CATIE collection was lost due to adaptation and virus problems (Alexander Stollberg, personal communication) and due to the survival of the duplicates at the two places in Nicaragua, it was possible to maintain the Central American collection, and a copy of the missing material was sent back to Costa Rica in 1986.

In the collection gardens, variability is maintained and there are no problems due to genetic changes of the material, but the maintenance cost per accession is high especially in the case of annual species. In most of the Third World countries, if the garden is big enough, it can be managed like an orchard and the produce sold, as uniformity requirements for the commercial product are not as stringent as in the industrialised countries. If enough land is available, it is even recommended that the living collection be managed as a farm or cooperative, under the technical supervision of the curator.

2.2 Seed Storage

The seed is the way in which plants survive most of the

time with a minimum of physiological activity. To a certain extent, it can be said that it is the way through which species store themselves. Therefore, the easiest way to store genetic resources is storing seeds.

For seed storage there are two general statements. Frankel (1970), Harrington (1970) and Bass (1979) consider that genetic resources should be stored sample by sample and in an independent manner. Other authors (Allard, 1970b; Hawkes, 1970) propose to join populations and work with composite populations. The difference in the two proposals can be seen in the possibility of the accession representing the original population for future use. If the main goal is the utilisation of genetic resources starting with a reality of the peasant, samples should not be mixed. Allard (1970b) and Frankel (1970) worry about the loss of characters when various accessions are joined. This problem can be found when certain characteristics of the population have low frequencies. During regeneration certain characteristics (for example, small plants) can be eliminated, consciously or unconsciously. Some examples will be seen on this in the chapter on regeneration. Fidel Marquez (Personal communication) proposed in 1965 that one should differentiate between the creation of composites for genetic breeding purposes and the conservation of genetic resources, which should be made without mixing accessions.

The general storage techniques have been described by Harrington (1970), Justice and Bass (1978) and Bass (1979). An English manual for the use of laboratory techniques was published by Hanson (1985), in which the main principles and procedures for the management of germplasm in a genetic resources laboratory are described.

2.2.1 Cooling System

For the storage of seeds one would need a coldroom. If the number of accession is small, a refrigerator or freezing cabinet will do. A coldroom generally has three areas: the coldroom itself, an antechamber and a machine room. The refrigeration system is based on refrigerating gas which is compressed and as it evaporates by passing through an expansion valve, will absorb heat and cool the air in the cooling circuit.

The following text describes the refrigeration system of a typical coldroom taking as a reference Figure VI.1.

The system is centred on a gas compressor, whose size will determine the temperature which can be reached and the air volume which can be cooled. At the exit from the compressor, the refrigerant is hot at high pressure and in gas form. It passes through an oil filter and afterwards enters a cooling coil which is cooled with air or water. The refrigerant exits the coil in liquid state (condensed) at high pressure and medium temperature. It then passes through a dehydrant, frequently in a bypass position, which allows the refrigerant to circulate directly to the second heat exchanger during normal functioning.

In this second heat exchanger, the liquid refrigerant is cooled by the cold gas which returns from the cooling coil to the compressor. The liquid refrigerant passes through this heat exchanger and arrives at the expansion valve. In the expansion valve, it passes from the liquid to the gas phase, thereby absorbing heat in the third heat exchanger or cooling coil. The air which surrounds the exchanger is cooled. Once the cooling coil is passed, the gas returns to the compressor, cooling on the way the liquid refrigerant in the second heat exchanger.

Some large refrigeration systems, through a relay which closes the solenoid valve 1 and opens the solenoid 2, activate a second gas circuit when the cooling coil gets covered with ice, or when the room has reached the desired temperature, or to avoid the overcharging of the equipment. This circuit injects hot gas directly to the coil, thawing the ice on it and the gas then returns again through the compressor's suction. Modern models generally thaw the coil through electric resistances.

Electric circuits must be protected with fuses and thermic breakers. The compressor is protected by three presiostats, one for low gas pressure, one for high gas pressure and one for minimum oil pressure. If any one of the

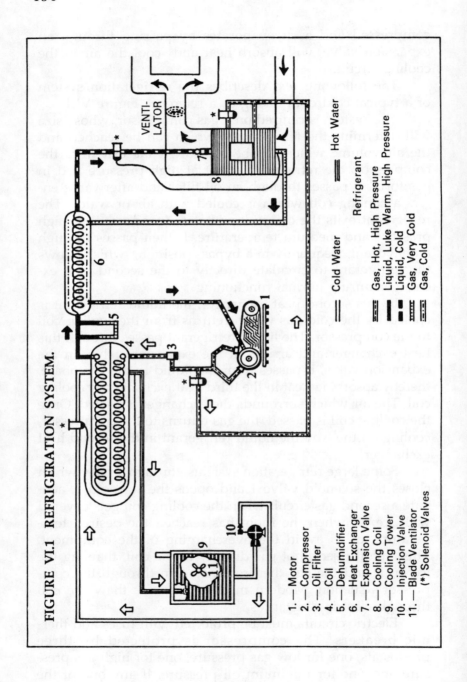

FIGURE VI.1 REFRIGERATION SYSTEM.

1. — Motor
2. — Compressor
3. — Oil Filter
4. — Coil
5. — Dehumidifier
6. — Heat Exchanger
7. — Expansion Valve
8. — Cooling Coil
9. — Cooling Tower
10. — Injection Valve
11. — Blade Ventilator
(*) Solenoid Valves

VENTI-LATOR

═══ Hot Water
═══ Cold Water
▓▓▓ Refrigerant

▓▓▓ Gas, Hot, High Pressure
▬▬▬ Liquid, Luke Warm, High Pressure
▬ ▬ Liquid, Cold
▪ ▪ ▪ Gas, Very Cold
░░░ Gas, Cold

presiostats jumps, the compressor is disconnected.

The system works with different gases like Freon 12 and Freon 22. With Freon 22, temperatures below -10°C can be attained as it has an evaporating pressure which is higher, at equal temperature, than Freon 12.

Cold air enters the chamber through a ventilator which sucks the air through the coil and injects it over the higher part of the chamber. Air recirculating ventilators inside of the room maintain a uniform temperature. An antechamber prevents hot air from getting in during entrances and exits.

The design of storage rooms for genetic resources has been described by Cromarty *et al.* (1985) and it can be adapted to the working conditions in the Third World, even though the proposed costs are higher than the real costs in the Third World and some of the elements may not be absolutely necessary.

2.2.2. *Evolution of seeds during storage*

When seeds are stored, depending on the temperature, humidity and initial germination characteristics, after a certain period they will lose their viability and vigour. This is the most significant change in seeds during storage. There are also other important changes for genetic resources.

The survival and therefore other variables related to the genetic composition of the stored material, will be influenced by a series of facts. James *et al.* (1976a and b) studied the survival differences of tomato, beans, peas, melons, cucumbers and sweet maize varieties as a function of storage. The experiment was made with 3 temperatures, 3 relative humidities, 5-8 varieties of each one of the species and 3 different harvest years. The germination tests showed significant differences in germination for all crops and all variables studied. This indicates the great variability in the survival of seeds. Roos (1979c) showed a significant superiority in the germination of seeds without pelletisation treatment after a relatively short period of storage, which means one should not pelletise or treat seeds with any chemicals.

There is a series of causes and effects in the aging of seeds during storage. In the following lines we will see the 3 types of changes which, according to Roos (1980), happen during storage: physiological changes, biochemical changes and genetic changes. One should remember that genetic and physiological changes are expression of biochemical ones.

Essential biochemical changes are the self-oxidising of lipids (fats) and the consequent weakening of the membranes, the reduction of enzyme activity (Roos, 1980), and a reduction in the repairing capacity of the cell walls due to lack of water for enzyme activity (Villiers, mentioned by Bass, 1975).

Physiological changes are basically the induction or loss of dormancy depending on the species and a change in the maximum temperature (cereals), minimum temperature (*Amaranthus spp.*) or both (*Quenopodiaceae*) for optimum germination. There is also the loss of seed vigour, which can have a marked effect on heterogeneous populations. Roos (1977a, 1977b, 1984a) studied the evolution of an artificial bean population made up of 8 varieties. After accelerated ageing (putting seeds in an oven at 32°C and a 90% relative humidity for 17 weeks) this mixture was measured for the presence of the different varieties during emergence. After 3 weeks of storage under the mentioned conditions, the proportion of each one of the varieties changed and at six weeks 3 of the 8 varieties which made up the mixture disappeared completely. This is evidently a big risk when one is working with genetic resources, as even before regeneration certain genotypes may have disappeared even if the sample is found to have a relatively high germination percent. However, Roos et al. (1982), in a similar experiment with *Dactilis glomerata*, did not observe systematic changes after storage, as height of plants, date of anthesis, number of spikes per plant and vigour, were not different in materials stored from 8-35 weeks at between 21°C and 38°C and between 50% and 90% relative humidity, when compared to the control.

The genetic changes during storage are frequently aberrations and in certain cases, mutations. In a series of articles, Murata, Tzuchiya and Roos (1977, 1978, 1979a, 1979b, 1981, 1982) analyse the effect of accelerated aging on the germination of barley. The correlation between the percentage of seed which did not germinate and the amount of aberrant anaphases was highly significant (r = .97). However, the longer the roots, the fewer aberrant cells were found, which is an indication that aberrations disappear with time.

Roos (1982) analysed the genetic changes caused by storage and arrived at the conclusion that the changes, even though statistically significant, did not really influence the genetic composition of the material. Onion seeds stored for six years were as normal as seeds with one year of storage and 80% germination (Harrison and McCleish, 1954, mentioned by Roos, 1982). On the other hand, the frequency of aberrant anaphases during the first mitosis was not higher than 5% of the studied cells even though the material had only 1% germination.

Another important phenomenon as shown by Roos (1982) can be seen in Figure VI.2. The percentage of aberrations after the first mitosis in seeds stored for a certain time, which only had 25% germination, decreased during the first three weeks until it reached, at meiosis state, only 2%. This is similar to the percentage of aberrations in plants starting with 85-99% germination. Finally, seeds which arose from plants with aberrations had the same level of aberrations as seeds produced by plants with normal percentage of aberrations. Based on this, even if there was a large number of aberrations, it would not have any negative effect on the storage and maintenance of genetic resources.

Mutations during storage are relatively infrequent. Generally, genotypes with mutations produce abortive pollen during flowering. Accumulated mutations are finally the cause of death for the seed.

Even though these changes happen during storage, the survival capacity of seeds is remarkable even under much

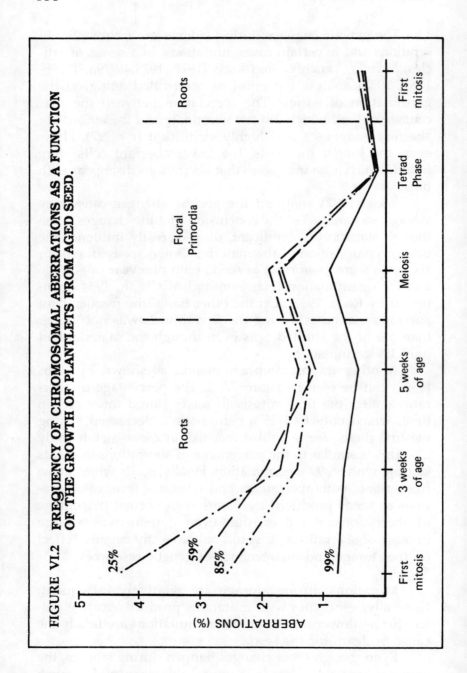

FIGURE VI.2   FREQUENCY OF CHROMOSOMAL ABERRATIONS AS A FUNCTION OF THE GROWTH OF PLANTLETS FROM AGED SEED.

worse storage conditions. Harrington (1970) published a table of survival of seeds stored in soil (Table VI.1), which was compiled based on a series of experiments and field data, which included the survival of seeds which had been found in burial sites. Without going to the extremes of storing seeds in soil, James *et al.* (1967b) studied the effect of intense temperature variations during storage on the germination of rye, soya, wheat and safflower seeds, storing the control at a low constant temperature and the treatments in a cycling temperature regime between -12°C and +32°C, which was repeated for 34 weeks. All the materials had the same germination percentage notwithstanding the pressure they were submitted to by the cyclic temperature variations. It is probable that this is due to the dormancy period which is induced by cold and is not deactivated quickly; therefore, the seed will not deteriorate even at relatively high temperatures, as long as they do not remain warm for a long period of time and the humidity does not increase.

Survival under better storage conditions has been reported by Justice and Bass (1978), Ellis and Roberts (1980a, b), Roberts and King (1981) and Ellis *et al.* (1982). In 1977, Roberts and Ellis proposed the use of a generalised equation to estimate the survival of seeds stored at temperatures below 0°C. This equation should have allowed the prediction of the percentage of living seeds as a function of storage temperature, moisture content, initial germination, days in storage and a certain number of specific constants which were calculated for barley, onion, beans, soya and *Vigna sp.* Murata *et al.* (1981) consider that the equation by Roberts did not really estimate the accelerated aging of barley but Murata *et al.* do not report how big the deviation from the predicted survival was. Moore and Roos (1982) proposed an alternative equation which was more simple. It will be necessary to compare both the equations to determine which is the best one and has the widest range of applications. For the time being, it would seem more adequate to make selective germination tests to determine the right moment to regenerate seeds.

Table VI.1   Survival of seeds in soil

Family	Genera and species	Survival(years)
Gramineae	Phalaris arundinacea	30
	Phleum pratense	21
	Poa pratensis	39
	Setaria lutescens	30
	Setaria viridis	39
Cyperaceae	Cyperus esculentus	21
Urticaceae	Boehmeria nivea	39
	Urtica dioica	600
Chenopodiaceae	Beta vulgaris	21
	Chenopodium album	1700
	Chenopodium hybridum	39
Caryophyllaceae	Cerastium caespitesum	600
	Spergula arvensis	1700
Ranunculaceae	Ranunculus repens	600
Amaranthaceae	Amaranthus retroflexus	40
Phytolaccaceae	Phytolacca americana	>39
Portulacaceae	Portulaca oleracea	40
Nymphaeaceae	Nelumbo nucifera	1000
Cruciferae	Brassica campestris	600
	Brassica nigra	50
Leguminosae	Lespedeza intermedia	>39
	Lupinus arcticus	1000
	Trifolium hybridum	30
	Trifolium pratense	>41
	Trifolium repens	600
Anacardiaceae	Rhus glabra	39
Umbelliferae	Apium graveolens	39
Convolvulaceae	Convolvulus sepium	>39
	Cuscuta polygonorum	39
	Ipomoea lacunosa	39
Verbenaceae	Verbena hastata	39
Labiatae	Glecoma hederacea	400
Solanaceae	Datura stramonium	>39
	Hyoscyamus niger	600
	Nicotiana tabacum	>39
	Solanum nigrum	>39
Plantaginaceae	Plantago mayor	40
Compositae	Ambrosia artemisiifolia	>39
	Arctium lappa	39
	Carduus crispus	600
	Chrysanthemum leucanthemum	39
	Helianthus annuus	30
	Taraxacum vulgare	600

Taken from Harrington (1970).

2.2.3. Regeneration

When seed has been stored for some time, its germination rate decreases and it is necessary to plant it in order to have new and vigorous seed. This process is called regeneration. There is a second case, multiplication, in which accessions are planted because the available seeds in the gene bank has been reduced, or when a very small sample arrives at the bank after collection, or through introduction from other genebanks. Both cases will be discussed simultaneously under the concept of regeneration, as even though the reasons for planting are different, the problems and methods are similar.

One of the critical phases in the management of genetic resources stored through seed is regeneration, especially in cross-pollinated plants. During regeneration, a series of changes can occur which affect the original composition of the accession. Regeneration will very often reduce variability in the sample. The regeneration differentiates itself if the species is self-pollinated or cross-pollinated and both cases will be looked at separately.

a) Self-pollinated (Autogamous):

Roos (1977a, 1979b, 1984b) mixed 8 bean varieties to create a synthetic heterogeneous accession with 8 components. This accession was artificially aged and regenerated for 3 cycles. Important changes in the proportion of each one of the components of the accession did occur. This was due partly to variability during emergence and the consequent relative survival of each one of the 8 components and to relative productivity, which varied from 0.62 to 1 between components. Considering that 6 factors which influence variability in a collection existed (Figure VI.3), these variables were included in a simulation model and the most important factor to maintain the components in an accession was defined to be the size of the sample. In a sample of 16 plants with 10 components there is a probability close to zero of maintaining all 10 initial components. On the other

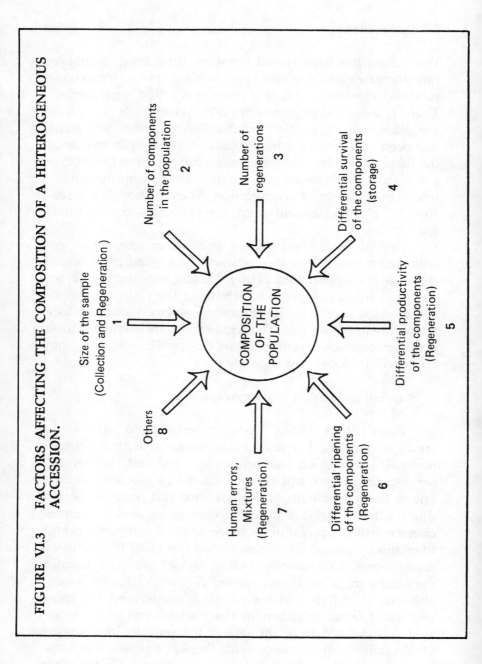

FIGURE VI.3   FACTORS AFFECTING THE COMPOSITION OF A HETEROGENEOUS
ACCESSION.

Size of the sample
(Collection and Regeneration)
1

Number of components
in the population
2

Number of
regenerations
3

Differential survival
of the components
(storage)
4

Differential productivity
of the components
(Regeneration)
5

Differential ripening
of the components
(Regeneration)
6

Human errors,
Mixtures
(Regeneration)
7

Others
8

COMPOSITION
OF THE
POPULATION

hand, even if one supposes there is a population of 64 plants, half of the components of the population would disappear due to regeneration over 15 cycles. In the long term, only one of the initial components would be left in the accession.

Roos (1979a) also separated accessions by seed colour, creating sub-groups. For each sub-group there was a remarkable variability in days to flowering, so that the risk exists that one would lose late material in the case of an early frost or early material in the case of a late harvest, as the seeds would have fallen to the ground. This example is mentioned because it is easy to know *a priori* that variability exists (colour differences); it is important to remember that variability exists even if it does not have such a clear expression as seed colour.

b) Cross-pollinated species (Alogamous):

What has just been mentioned is also valid for alogamous species and new factors appear, which have also to be taken into consideration. One must ensure that the plants from which one expects to get seeds will be pollinated by other plants of the same accession; that there will be enough male plants in the case of dioecious (plants which have male and female flowers on different plants) species; that the insect-pollinated species be visited; and in the worst case, pollination will be manual. Goplen *et al.* (1972) studied the effect of isolation distance on the contamination of certified clover seeds. They concluded that the isolation distances which were recommended for seed production were not enough and that there can be a 20% contamination after 4 multiplications.

The way to get good pollination is through dense isolated population of the same accession, with mesh boxes for each one, or through the recollection of pollen in bags and applying of this on the flowers of interest (this is a specific technique for some species) or otherwise by individual flower pollination techniques which are generally tedious and labour intensive.

Seeing the limitations and difficulties which arise during regeneration, it is clear that sufficient seeds of good quality from each accession should be collected to ensure their immediate entrance to the seedbank. The reduction in germination percent should also be very carefully decided, in order to justify regeneration procedures. Roos (1982) concludes that it is not worthwhile regenerating when the germination gets 5%-10% lower than the initial germination, as IBPGR recommends (IBPGR, 1979). This is because no significant changes in the structure of the population due to germination reduction do occur and these changes can be caused at a much larger scale during regeneration. As the regeneration costs in personnel, time, and material involved are very high, it should only be done when absolutely necessary. Based on those criteria, it is reasonable to regenerate seeds which have gone down to 60% of the initial germination, trying to work with as large populations as possible during regeneration.

Regeneration should also be used in order to have a better characterisation of the material and for certain basic evaluation.

2.3. Storage through tissue culture

The storage in tissue culture is relatively new. It is the keeping of accessions in glass containers (*in vitro*) in an artificial environment, basically an inert substrate (Agar), salts, various nutrients and hormones, which with an adequate management, allow the slow growth of a plantlet or a specific tissue.

The germplasm maintenance costs in the field are frequently very high and include risks of losses due to natural phenomena and human errors. This is even more difficult when one tries to keep copies of crops outside of their usual environment, which is very important for certain temperate countries which have interests in the tropical commodities markets. (Methods for cocoa *in vitro* storage are being looked for in England).

Withers (1980 and 1981) analysed the potential of tissue culture techniques for the maintenance of genetic resources, and concluded that even though there were a certain biological contamination problems in species of *Theobroma, Dioscorea, Colocasia* and *Solanum* and that there were management problems in 14 of the species stored with tissue culture, either due to instability of the agar medium during transport or totipotency of plants after having been stored in normal growth medium, in many cases there were positive results. Many species had not been studied until then and it was probable that storage and multiplication through tissue culture would be possible. Withers (1981) concluded that it was very probable that the biological problems which were described until then could be surmounted.

In order to store germplasm *in vitro*, the first step is to develop an adequate medium for its growth. However, very soon the problem of excessive growth of the plant in the test-tubes arises, which makes it necessary to transplant them frequently. In the last few years, Schilde-Rentschler and Schmiediche (1984) reported of media which allow the growth of potato plantlets in the same test-tube for two years. Not in all crops have such good results been achieved.

In 1988, there were very few crops for which the appropriate medium for *in vitro* growth is unknown. For many asexually reproduced crops there are *in vitro* germplasm banks, as for example the world potato collection in the International Potato Centre in Peru, in Holland and the United States; the world collection of cassava in International Tropical Agriculture Centre (Colombia) and partial collections of sweet potato and Andean root crops in Peru; of sugarcane in Cuba and Trinidad and Tobago; of *Colocasia, Xanthosoma* and vanilla in Costa Rica and bananas in the Philippines.

Tissue culture has helped to transfer genetic resources, reducing the risk of transporting simultaneously insects and diseases, from the centre of origin to the international banks (Withers and Williams, 1985). A case which serves as a good example has been the transfer of the potato collection which was stored at the International Potato Centre in Peru to Holland and the United States. Presently, a similar collection, in this case of sweet potato, is also being sent to the United States (!).

2.4 Cryopreservation

The storage at ultra-low temperatures (-196ºC, the temperature of liquid nitrogen) can be used for seeds and pollen as well as for isolated cells and tissues.

The effect of low temperatures on plant and animal cells has been studied over the last 100 years, due to the interest in producing frost-resistant plants. Olien (1967) and Burke *et al.* (1976) reviewed the literature on the subject and some of their conclusion can be applied to genetic resources conservation. When seeds are stored at temperatures which are not below -40ºC, frequently the cells are maintained in a state of super-cooling, in which there is still liquid water, without the formation of ice, due to the absence of a nucleus for the formation of ice or due to the existence of high concentrations of molecules in solution which does not allow the water to freeze. In the case of pure water, for example, one can go down to -38ºC without ice formation, in the absence of nucleating substances. Super-cooling is possible in certain cells of developed tissues at -47ºC, but the formation of intracellular ice is lethal afterwards, as the crystals damage the cell walls (Burke *et al.*, 1976). In seeds stored at -40 ºC there is no ice formation due to the low water content of the same.

Storage at temperatures below -40ºC is based on the formation of ice, in such a way that it will not damage the cells inside or around which the water is found. There are 2 basic procedures for the storage at ultra-low temperatures:

1) Very rapid cooling (500 to 1500ºC per second) with ice formation inside of the cells. The crystals will be very small and will therefore not damage the cells walls and tissues.

2) Gradual cooling of the tissue, with simultaneous dehydration. At the end of this process, cells at temperatures below -80ºC and without internal ice formation are obtained. The crystals are outside of the cell walls and there is therefore no risk of death of the cells.

Both techniques have been tried with many species, from isolated cells all the way to complex tissues, plants and seeds. The first technique is used mainly for the storage of seeds, in which the crystals will be small due to the quick descent of temperature and the low moisture contents of the seed. The second technique is used for tissues with a high water content, as the risk of ice formation which will perforate the cell walls is greater. This technique is used with tissue culture.

2.4.1. Seeds

Experiments on seed storage at ultra-low temperature are relatively recent. Therefore, there are no conclusive reports as to the effect of such temperatures on the long term. Stanwood and Roos (1979) conducted three experiments to see the effects of ultra-low temperature storage on horticultural seeds. 14 vegetable species and 2 of flowers were not damaged after 6 months storage in liquid nitrogen. Four bean varieties stored for 7 days in liquid nitrogen did not lose their vigour. Lastly, seeds of snap peas stored in liquid nitrogen for 30 days and a similar batch heated and cooled from 23°C to -196°C 15 times in 1 month did not change their germination percentage. On top of that, the alternating temperature treatment broke dormancy. In the case of lettuce seed there was some damage, as it had a high moisture contents (14 to 20%).

Stanwood (1980) studied the tolerance of 29 crops to liquid nitrogen storage for 6 months. Only flax and sesame were damaged during storage. All the other species, even those with relatively high moisture content (maize, 8.5%) maintained their initial germination percentage. Stanwood and Bass (1981) compiled a list of 120 species stored at -196°C, for which there was no negative effect on germination and mentioned the advantages of this technique which saves electricity and will probably allow storage of seeds for much longer periods, thereby avoiding regeneration.

Stanwood (1980) used a cooling technique by induction into liquid nitrogen, which gave a cooling speed of 200 to 400°C per minute. Stanwood and Bass (1981) tested a series of cooling rhythms, which depended on the container in which the seed was placed. With canned seeds, the cooling speed was 5 to 15°C per minute; in glass jars it was 20 to 30°C per minute and in laminated foil envelopes 200°C per minute. Thawing through exposure to air temperature (10-15°C) allowed an adequate heating at a rate of 10 to 15°C per minute. Thawing with luke warm water is not equally efficient, probably because it is too fast.

2.4.2 Storage of cells, tissues and pollen

In the case of large tissues the technique of freezing outside of the cells is used and in the case of pollen the formation of small ice crystals inside the cell is used.

The first technique is based on dehydrating with products which absorb the water inside the cell (cryoprotectants). These substances have a similar effect to what happens in the seed during ripening. Examples of these cryoprotectants are dimethyl-sulfoxide and glycerol.

Freezing is done at a rather slow rate (0.1°C per minute) and simultaneously water is extracted from the inside of the cells through increasingly higher concentrations of cryoprotectant.

For quick freezing, the most common way is to immerse the tissue directly or within an ampule in liquid nitrogen. This allows us to obtain typical cooling rates of 1000 to 2000°C per minute. A description of the typical cooling and thawing techniques is shown in Figure VI.4, taken from Withers (1980). Once the tissues are at temperatures below -70°C, it is easy to store them over long periods of time.

The technique which is generally used for thawing is the immersion of tissues in water at 40°C. Tissues treated this way grow well. Sometimes there are de-plasmolysis problems, due to the loss of membrane surface during dehydration and because in certain cases ice crystals pierce the cell walls. The dead cells in a tissue can cause contamination

FIGURE VI.4
FREEZING (1-6) AND THAWING (7 AND 8)
PROTOCOLS FOR THE STORAGE OF CELLS AND
PLANT TISSUES AT ULTRA-LOW TEMPERATURES.
TAKEN FROM WITHERS (1980).

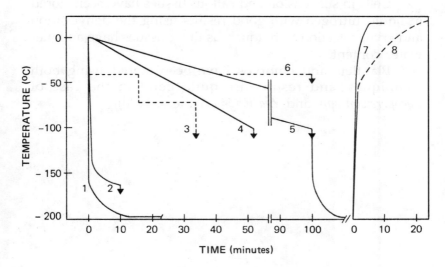

1. Very quick freezing obtained by submerging of the specimen in liquid nitrogen.
2. Quick freezing, obtained keeping the specimen above liquid nitrogen. The slope of the curve would stepen by reducing the distance between the specimen and liquid nitrogen.
3. Step by step freezing. The steps will be steep as the graph shows in the case of small specimens or less steep in the case of larger specimens.
4. Slow cooling at 2 °C per minute.
5. Slow cooling at 1 °C per minute.
6. Slow cooling, with a stabilising period at an intermediate temperature.
7. Quick thawing, for example in water 35 to 40 °C.
8. Slow thawing, for example in air at room temperature.
The arrows show the end of the cooling and beginning of the final phase, by a transfer into liquid nitrogen.

problems as toxins are produced which may damage the undamaged cells.

The results have been good in the case of pollen which, due to its low water content, reacts well to storage at -196°C with quick freezing without the need of cryoprotectants.

Cells in suspension and callous tissues have been stored in liquid nitrogen with good results using the dehydration and cryoprotection techniques, as these tissues have a higher water content.

Plantlets and embryos have been stored using both techniques, and results are quite good in the case of *Lycopersicon spp.* and *Zea mays* (Withers, 1980).

Characterization of the Nicaraguan collection of cassava
(*Manihot esculenta*) in Managua.

VII
Characterization and Evaluation

GENETIC RESOURCES are collected for use in breeding programmes, and not only to be preserved. In all cases, it is not enough to have the seeds or the plants but one must also have the information on them. Minimum information which one should have for each accession are the passport descriptors taken during collection.

It is necessary to increase knowledge about the accession and therefore, data is obtained in two phases. The first phase is **characterisation**, when data which describe each accession is taken, in order to know if it is a separate race or which characteristics differentiate it from other accessions. The second phase is **evaluation;** when one obtains all the data of immediate interest on the collection. Evaluation will be different in the case of potential species or conventional species.

1. DESCRIPTORS LIST DEVELOPMENT

Theoretically, the amount of data which can be taken during characterisation and evaluation is infinite, but a good and useful plant description will not be determined by the number of described variables but by the practical use of these and their precision. Therefore, in practice the data obtained will be limited to useful characteristics for the breeding or use of the plants or for knowledge of the population structure of the species. Before starting to plant in order to describe an accession, the data to be taken has to be defined, that is to say the descriptor list or catalogue has to be formulated.

1.1. Terms and Importance

When one works with genetic resources, the word "descriptor" is used to define a characteristic or an attribute which one can observe in the accessions within a genebank. Examples of descriptors are plant height, flower colour, days to flowering, number of seeds per pod, common name, etc. The "descriptor states" are the values which a descriptor can have in specific cases, like, continuing with the aforementioned examples, 140 cm. height, red flower, 96 days to flowering, 6 seeds per pod, "popcorn", etc.

Howes (1981) proposes to differentiate four levels of information on a collection:

a) Passport information. This information is basic as described in the chapter on collections, and includes the accession number.

b) Characterization data. This includes easily observable botanic characteristics with qualitative inheritance generally. The curator takes care that this data be taken during multiplication or regeneration. Certain characteristics can be taken during the collection stage, as for example, colour of the ripe fruit or the flowers' characteristics.

c) Preliminary Evaluation. This data relates to agronomic or other characteristics, which will be defined by the consensus of users (plant breeders, botanists, peasants, etc.) of the species. These characteristics generally will be easy to measure and can also be taken during multiplication or regeneration of the seeds.

d) Further evaluation. This data directly relates to breeding programmes under execution. They include theoretically, an unlimited number of characteristics. This type of evaluation will generally be made by the user of the sample and should not be a direct responsibility of the genebank. When there are no immediate users of the collection (as in the case of non-conventional species), specific research lines should allow one to take evaluation all the way to this level. It is important because the existence of full information on potential breeding will determine the future use of the collection in a dialectic manner, changing with time according to the needs.

The descriptor list for a species is all the descriptors of the aforementioned categories which allows one to rationalise the data taken in the field during characterization and evaluation. It also enables one to compare information between people who evaluate plants under different conditions.

Researchers, especially in industrialised countries, who have precise objectives in their own breeding programmes, frequently under the auspices of IBPGR, have elaborated descriptor lists for known or semi-conventional species (see Appendix III).

Descriptor lists should be analysed by the curators and discussed with the users in each country to adapt them to the information needs, selecting the most adequate descriptors.

If an already elaborated descriptor list is not available for the species of interest, the person in charge of evaluation, together with the users of germplasm, should define the variables to be studied. In the following discussion, we will see the procedure to elaborate a descriptor list, using as a base the scheme presented by Howes (1981).

1.2. Definition of Descriptors

Descriptors must be clear for those working with a crop, taking into account the different uses of the crop, the different breeding objectives and the different measuring techniques for a certain characteristic, as well as the variability of the species. Each descriptor must represent only one characteristic and it should be defined at which growth stage of the plant data should be taken.

The number of times a measurement should be made on a plant is one of the most difficult variables to define when one starts to work with a species, as the missing knowledge on the variability of a characteristic makes it impossible to define the adequate sample size to estimate the mean. The same problem arises in the determination of the number of plants which should be described for each accession. Commonly, four measurements will be made per plant in the case of an unknown variability within the plant, and the data will be taken on 20 plants to estimate the variability between plants of the same accession. The estimated variance with the obtained data allows one to adjust the number of measurements per plant and per accession in order to have a known precision and error margin.

1.2.1. Definition of Descriptors States

Three types of descriptors can be differentiated according to the states they can assume:

a) Descriptors which assume alphabetic values, different for each collection. There are few restrictions in the possible state of the descriptors, for example, place of collection, species, name of the collector, etc. and are not often used in characterisation.

b) Descriptors with a limited number of states (discreet, discontinuous or qualitative), for example, the colour of the seeds in maize can take the values white, yellow, red and purple and combinations; or the presence or absence of a character.

c) Descriptors which states have a numerical value and a continuous range of values (continuous or quantitative), for example yield per hectare. They can be subdivided into two groups: those in which the observed value is registered and those which are coded based on numeric ranges. It is correct to store this continuous descriptors keeping the measures in grams, days or centimetres when the measurement is done in different environments or on enough plants to ensure accurate and representative mean and variance.

If one cannot ensure accuracy, a fourth type of descriptor should be used. For example, days to flowering of the accessions studied can be compared to the days to flowering of the commercial or standard variety, and therefore the classification can be as "very early", "intermediate" or "very late maturing", as related to that reference variety.

When lengths or shapes are measured, it should be clearly defined between which points that measurement has to be made, if possible including a diagram and the measurement units.

When weights are to be measured, be it directly or indirectly, it must be clearly established if the weight is fresh or dry weight, or of material with a certain humidity percentage.

Colour descriptors should be expressed with words for the most common colours to be found in the species, and referred to a standard colour table, as colour perception will vary from person to person and country to country. These tables are unfortunately expensive and difficult to obtain, but colour atlas or colour guides for artists can be used. In the worst case, colour samples from paint companies can be used to ensure the criterion uniformity within a group of people.

1.2.2. How to Choose Codes

The codes for descriptors state should, whenever possible, follow a logical order. When a certain characteristic does not exist, it should be coded as zero, and if the data does not exist, has not been taken or has been lost, the field is left empty or with a unique code for all cases, as for example a cross. The importance of this differentiation lies in the fact that, for example, it is not the same to say that the plant grows no roots to saying that they have not been counted.

Descriptors which are not stored in their measurement units but are formally described, must be taken on a scale from 1 to 9. The codes, independently of the number of states the descriptor has, should be seen as a reduction of the following codes:

Code	State
0	Absence
1	Very low
2	Very low to low

3	Low
4	Low to intermediate
5	Intermediate
6	Intermediate to high
7	High
8	High to very high
9	Very high
+	Inexisting data

Taking as an example the case of potato, from Huaman *et al.* (1977) (Figure VII.1): Secondary flesh colour distribution.

0	Absent (Flesh only one colour)
1	Diffuse spots
2	Diffuse areas
3	Narrow vascular ring
4	Broad vascular ring
5	Vascular ring and center
6	Whole flesh, except the center
7	Others
+	Inexisting data

For some characteristics, the consensus of users will say that there are fewer than 9 observable levels in practice, for example:

Stem   width

3	Thin
5	Intermediate
7	Wide
+	Unavailable data

The codes 3, 5, 7 are used to allow for intermediate values. Whoever does not agree with this coding, can use, for example, the code 1 (very thin) and 9 (very wide) and in the case of a doubt between narrow and intermediate, code 4 can be used.

Dates should always be expressed numerically. It is

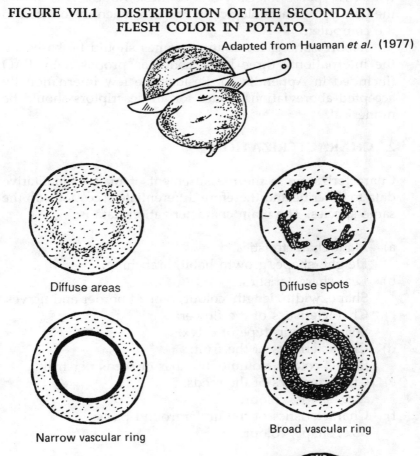

FIGURE VII.1   DISTRIBUTION OF THE SECONDARY FLESH COLOR IN POTATO.

Adapted from Huaman *et al.* (1977)

Diffuse areas

Diffuse spots

Narrow vascular ring

Broad vascular ring

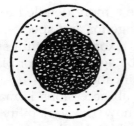

Vascular ring and center

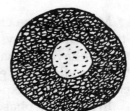

Whole flesh, except the center

recommended that the date be written as year, month, day, with two spaces for each one of these values. This allows the data to be chronologically ordered when introduced to the computer.

Abbreviations for country names should be based on the international three letter codes as proposed by FAO (included in Appendix II). Besides the few internationally accepted abbreviations, codes for all descriptors should be numerical.

2. CHARACTERIZATION

Characterization is the measurement of mainly qualitative data to describe and therefore differentiate accessions of the same species. The main characterization data is:

a) Plant characteristics:
    Height, shape, growth habit, branching.
b) Leaf characteristics:
    Shape, width, length, colour, type of border and nerves.
c) Characteristics of the flower:
    Shape, colour, type of calyx.
d) Characteristics of the fruit:
    Shape, colour, volume, number of seeds per fruit.
e) Characteristics of the seeds:
    Size, shape, colour.
f) Characteristics of the underground parts:
    Size, shape, colour.

Many of these characteristics are a more detailed form of the taxonomic keys to differentiate genus and species. As botanists have not worked much on taxonomy within species, these efforts are generally made by agronomists or plant breeders without experience in classification.

In the first phase, the study of all accessions is made and characterization allows us to know the variability of the genera. As an example, one could take the work by Hawkes (1944), who characterized potato collections of Mexico and South America. The classification of the samples and their cytological study, allowed the rewriting of a taxonomic key which showed the existence of new species and to generate a blueprint of the evolution of tuberous species of the genus *Solanum*.

Whitaker and Knight (1980) collected cucurbits in Mexico and based on a first characterisation established the existence of 22 collections of the genus *Cucurbita* which had not been described in the literature, which presented the possibility of new species being there.

In the case of non-conventional species, it is necessary to first establish the characteristic which will be useful for the classification of the genus or the species under study. Respecting the rules for descriptor list elaboration and based on the descriptor lists for similar genera or species, a descriptor guide is elaborated which is used for the first test.

Data is taken from this first guide, which is generally quite extensive. The analysis will reduce the number of descriptors necessary to differentiate the samples and determine the descriptors which are repetitive. If one takes chayote as an example, there are three main fruit colours which are significantly different between accessions. No significant differences between accessions were found for colour of the flower, and therefore for future characterisation it is recommended not to take that descriptor (Cruz and Querol, 1985).

3. EVALUATION

Evaluation criteria are based on the use of the crop and the characteristics which have been identified in order to make it better: generally higher yielding, easier to cultivate and more resistant to pests. Yield evaluation are similar to varietal tests for the species. Ideal agronomic characteristics will be determined by the peasants, consumers, and phytopathologists and breeders, who will consider the need to evaluate, for example, the behaviour of a plant under low input conditions.

Resistance to pests is a more complex problem to

evaluate. All plants are susceptible to diseases and insects, with a dependence on the environment in which they grow. Pests and traditional varieties co-evolve naturally, not so with the modern-bred varieties. That is why more variability can be found in the first than in the latter. The use of genetic resources to incorporate pest resistance in modern varieties is needed in any breeding programme. Resistance to pests should not only be evaluated for current, widely-distributed pests, but should also be evaluated for resistance to pests with relatively low aggressiveness at present. It is therefore necessary to have a collection of identified pests, which will be used to innoculate the crops during evaluation.

Hooker (1977) considers that in industrialised countries it is necessary to create genebanks specifically directed to pathogen resistance. These banks will allow a rapid reaction to the evolution of new pathogens and have sources of resistance available for the immediate use. It is clear that the plant resources will have to come from the Third World.

3.1 Non-conventional species

Over the last few years, there has been increased interest on non-conventional species work (NAS, 1975; NAS, 1979; Richie, 1979) and it is submitted that more systematic work on these species is necessary before they disappear. Evaluation of non-conventional species includes studies previous to those which are used for conventional ones.

Taking the example of some of the plants mentioned in the afore-mentioned publications, one can see the steps which will be needed for the evaluation of a non-conventional crop.

The genus *Amaranthus* has been used since pre-Colombian times as a food in most of the American continent due to its excellent food characteristics. After taking it to Europe as an ornamental plant, the Spanish colonialists banned its cultivation in Mexico as it was related to non-Christian rites. Peasants in Mexico continue using it, but with very little support from researchers. Many ecotypes and important varieties must have been lost, but now its importance as a food source has been rediscovered. In India and Africa, it is used as a vegetable, and in America the possibility exists to use *Amaranthus hipocondriatus* (synonymous to *Amaranthus retroflexus*) and *Amaranthus caudatus* widely as food crops.

An evaluation of this non-conventional food species can be made at three levels:

a)   Agronomic Characteristics.

It is necessary to know the agronomic characteristics of the species with which one is working, establishing experimental plots in which the useful (seed) yield of each accession is evaluated. If possible, crops which this species is supposed to replace (wheat, maize) should be planted simultaneously. The evaluation of yield will allow to measure the existing variability and estimate the potential for new samples to increase that variability.

b)   Food Characteristics

It is necessary to analyse the content and composition of amino acids, proteins in general, carbohydrates, fats and vitamins. If the plant contains amino acids which are not abundant in other crops, and of importance to the human diet, the species would become more important. As in the case of agronomic characteristics, evaluation will allow us to see the available variability and based on that to determine the maximum potential of each one of the evaluated characteristics.

c)   Real Potential of the Species

It is necessary to evaluate the real potential of the species, which is determined by the acceptance for human consumption and the marketing potential.

In the case of an industrial species there are some differences.

Guayule (*Partenium argentatum*) is a plant which grows in the arid zones in the north of Mexico and south of the United States. Its potential as a rubber source is known since 1852. At the beginning of this century, 50% of the rubber in the United States came from guayule produced in Mexico (CONACYT, 1981). In the early 1950's, with the introduction of synthetic rubber, the production of guayule dropped to almost zero. The presence of undesirable resins in guayule rubber almost completely eliminated it from the market. Later, the interest in the species was revived with the escalating oil price. An evaluation work on this resource should take the following parameters into account:

Even though there is profuse flowering, guayule seeds have low germination percentage, marked dormancy and little vigour. The evaluation should select plants with better seeds. Its agronomic characteristics have not been clearly defined even though work was made in the emergency military programme for rubber in the United States from 1930 to 1940. Ideal fertilising and irrigation techniques and the necessary cycle to obtain good production should be studied in more detail. The problems of destructive harvesting techniques currently used (extraction of the plants with roots and the rest) make it necessary to study the possibility of harvesting through superficial cutting in order to utilise the development of roots under difficult conditions. This would allow the regrowth of the plant, instead of replanting. It would be necessary to study if, between the accessions, there are some with a good percentage of regrowth, which would also solve the problem of seed quality because replanting would not be necessary each time.

Finally, in theory, guayule plants under environmental stress (low humidity, high temperatures, little nutrients) should have a higher rubber production. In practice, it was discovered that guayule plant under good irrigation conditions have produced more rubber than those under stress. One should therefore look for accessions which respond adequately to field conditions in the desert.

To make a general statement on an evaluation, it is necessary to consider two important steps: firstly, define **how** the evaluation is to be carried out, and secondly, **what** is to be evaluated.

In non-conventional species, the **how** is defined as a consequence of pre-existing knowledge on the planting needs, planting densities, date of fertiliser applications and doses (if it is necessary), the irrigation (if necessary), date and techniques for harvesting and post-harvest management.

What to be evaluated will depend on the goals for the final use of the species. For example, if one is looking for a new source of oil it will be necessary to discuss with people working on oil crops as to the necessary characteristics of oil-producing plants in order to establish a list of descriptors. The last step in an evaluation is the analysis of the results for their interpretation and publication.

4. ANALYSIS OF THE EVALUATION INFORMATION

When one evaluates, the amount of information generated is immense. A. Cruz (1983, personal communication) proposed an evaluation programme of 90 chayote accessions, which generated half a million data items to be analysed. In these conditions, it is absolutely necessary to use computers and statistical methods to get some conclusions out of this mass of information.

Analysis techniques for information generated through evaluation can go from descriptive graphs and procedures for the publication of catalogues of general use, all the way to multivariate statistical analysis and modelling. Different levels will be looked at in the following paragraphs.

Miller *et al.* (1982a) presents the simplest analysis of a collection in the case of flax (*Linum usitatissimum*), in which 4 characteristics of direct use by breeders were evaluated, correlations were made between the evaluation variables and Chi-square tests to determine if some type of direct relation existed between the geographical origin of the accession and the studied characters.

Tolbert *et al.* (1979) analysed the world barley collection from 3 points of view. First, they determined the percentage of accessions from the different regions and countries of the world and found that certain barley characters are concentrated in specific areas. Then, they analysed the variability for each one of these characters in each country and region, using the following variability index:

$$H' = -\sum_{i=1}^{n} P_i \log P_i$$

Where:

H' = Shannon-Weaver variability index

n = number of classes for each characteristic

P_i = proportion of individuals in the class i, in a char acteristic of n classes.

Based on this index, they proposed the existence of high variability areas which would be the equivalent of possible centres of origin. The third analysis was a Chi-square test on the collections to determine if within the available collections a strong link for the studied characteristics could be found.

In a not less interesting, but more conventional study, Davids (1980) evaluated the 362 accessions of the world collection of *Phaseolus lunatus* (lima bean) taking into account 80 descriptors. The objectives of the evaluation were the following:

● Identify and remove the duplicates

● Establish the total variability of the species studying all the plant types of the species.

● Study the correlation of characters observing the maximum number of characters simultaneously.

● Determine the phenotypic similarity coefficients between the plant types to enable their better usage during breeding programmes.

● Join the natural entities in order to reconstitute, for example, groups of cultivars and establish phylogenetic relationships.

To achieve these objectives, it was necessary to include descriptors which even though not a priority needed by breeding programmes, could serve other objectives. Once the data was taken, the following analysis were made:

Variability analysis was made on the variability coefficient for continuous variables. Those which had relatively low variability were excluded from further analysis, as they were not useful to differentiate collections.

The simple correlation matrix was calculated for related characteristics, so as to reduce the number of descriptors really needed.

Regression analysis for the yield components establishes which variables are most important for yield and their consistency.

Through the analysis of the frequency distribution of descriptor states, it was possible to define if there was marked variability. This was simultaneously studied in a table where countries or zones of origin of the collection were included in order to see which areas had more variability.

Factorial analysis was used to reach similar conclusions to those established by the correlation matrix, that is to say, the elimination of certain variables which could be defined by others.

Mehra (1981) considers that analysis should be made at 2 levels. First, one should determine the variability within each collection and afterwards analyse the characteristics and variability between collections. The variability and characteristics may be studied for one or more characters.

The use of one character alone makes interpretations easier and simple histograms or distribution curves to differentiate populations can be drawn. The analysis of two or more characters is made through partial correlations, factorial analysis and later the use of diagrams to represent co-variance of the two characters.

Finally, an important conclusion to which it is necessary to reach requires the determination of taxonomic groups at the level of races or varietal groups. In order to achieve this, one will work with groups of variables, using cluster analysis or taxonomic distance analysis, which allows comparisons of a large number of means because the usual techniques to group means (Duncan, Tukey, Shefeo tests) are not valid when more than 30 or 40 means are compared. In the case of genetic resources, the number of means to be compared is generally higher.

Work by Williams *et al.* (1980), Robinson *et al.* (1980) and Burt *et al.* (1980) are examples of the taxonomic distance techniques. In this series of articles, the study of the relationship between variables taken during evaluation and the area of the collection of the material is stated. This is achieved through the calculation of the similarity of certain samples, and calculation of distance matrices for the phenotypic characteristics. Then, the simplified distance matrix and the geographical location are plotted one on top of the another and big groups with common characteristics are established. Finally, one can compare the characteristics within the collecting area. Robinson *et al.* (1980) could not define agronomic characteristics based on isozyme analysis, but did find a good way to establish groups by collection zones.

This technique can be used to determine similar groups of collections. Once these groups are established, they will have to be studied in more detail to find phylogenetic relationships which exist within as well as between different groups for their use in interspecific crosses, essentially for introduction of resistance from wild species into cultivated plants.

All these analyses should not only simplify work within the genebank, by reducing the number of duplicate accessions, but should mainly lead to the utilisation of the results for practical field work. Once selected materials is found to be better, the distribution process of the materials should start immediately.

Opinion

THE THIRD WORLD stores the most important resources on earth. It does not only have populations but also the longest history and the deepest cultural roots which gave the rest of the world its material and philosophical bases. And we are still giving them away while our people die of hunger and diseases.

This book has only covered a small fraction of our potential: genetic resources created by nature in our space and by our forefathers.

We have two possibilities. We either take the decision of using our resources in solidarity and a nationalist attitude which should go beyond our borders and the defence of our rights, **or** we remain apathetic to the increasing poverty we are facing.

We must know that when a plant explorer from the North comes to us and we help him to take a small seed (which he may thank us possibly by inviting us for lunch), it is probable that we will be making a gift to the industrialised country of thousands or maybe even millions of dollars a year. This gift belongs to all the people who selected, planted, nurtured and harvested those plants for thousands of years.

Technically, the problem is simple. The mechanisms for

collection, conservation and utilisation of genetic resources can be started without the need for big investments, as has been shown in Nicaragua, where in the middle of a war the Nicaraguan genetic resources programme was initiated. Now, 7 years later, there is even a functioning tissue culture laboratory where the sleeping quarters of Somoza's National Guard were 10 years ago.

If we do not forget that the work on genetic resources and genebanks is only valid if, on top of preserving, it also helps to better the quality and quantity of useful products from and for our people, the potential we have in our hands will serve as base material for the change which is needed.

REFERENCES

Aosa, (1981), "Rules for testing seeds.", J. Seed Technology 6:1-126.

Allard, R.W., (1970a),"Population Structure and Sampling Methods.", In: Frankel, O.H. and Bennett, E. (EdS.), (1970), *Genetic Resources in Plants*. IBP Handbook No. 11, Blackwell Sc. Pub., pp. 97-107.

Allard, R.W., (1970b),"Problems of maintenance.", In: Frankel, O.H. and Bennett, E. (EdS.), (1970), *Genetic Resources in Plants*. IBP Handbook No. 11, Blackwell Sc. Pub., pp. 491-494.

Andrews, C.J. and Burrows, (1972),"Germination response of dormant seeds to low temperature and giberellin.", Can. J. Plant Sci. 52:295-303.

Arora, R.K., (1981),"Plant genetic resources exploration and collection. Planning and Logistics.", In: Mehra, K.L. *et al.* (1981), pp. 46-54.

Azurdia, C., (1980),"Estudio de las malezas en valles centrales de Oaxaca.", M.Sc. Thesis, Colegio de Postgraduados, Chapingo, Mexico.

Bailey, N.N., (1977),"Proceedings of the First Amaranth Seminar.", Rhodale Press, New Organic Gardening Experimental Farm, Maxatawny, Pennsylvania.

Bass, L.N., (1973),"Controlled atmosphere and seed storage.", Seed Sci. & Technol. 1:463-492.

Bass, L.N., (1975),"Seed moisture and storage.", Seed Sci. & Technol. 3:743-746.

Bass, L.N., (1978),"Sealed storage of crimson clover seed.", Seed Sci. & Technol. 6:1017-1024.

Bass, L.N., (1979),"Physiological and other aspects of seed preservation.", In: Rubenstein, I. (Ed.), *The plant seed*. pp. 145-170.

Bass, L.N. and Stanwood, P.C., (1978),"Long-term preservation of sorghum seed as affected by seed moisture, temperature and atmospheric environment.", Crop Sci. 18:575-577.

Bass, L.N., Clark, D.C. and James, E., (1963),"Vacuum and inert-gas storage of Safflower and Sesame seeds.", Crop Sci. 3:237-240.

Bennett, E., (1970),"Tactics of Plant Exploration.", In: Frankel, O.H. and Bennett, E. (Eds.), (1970), *Genetic Resources in Plants*. IBP Handbook No. 11, Blackwell Sc. Pub., pp. 157-179.

Bewley, J.D., (1979),"Dormancy breaking by hormones and other chemicals-Action at the molecular level.", In: Rubenstein, I. (Ed.), *The plant seed*. pp. 219-239.

Boyd, A.H., (1978),"Secamiento y acondicionamiento de semillas.", In: Boyd, A.H. and Echandi, R.Z. (Eds.), (1978), *Memorias del seminario int. sobre tecnologia de semillas para Centroamerica...*, pp. 148-162.

Boyd, A.H. and Cabrera, E., (1978),"Equipo comunmente utilizado en la limpieza de semillas.", In: Boyd, A.H. and Echandi, R.Z. (Eds.), (1978), *Memorias del seminario int. sobre tecnologia de semillas para Centroamerica...*, pp. 163-180.

Boyd, A.H. and Echandi, R.Z. (Eds.), (1978),"Memorias del Seminario Internacional sobre Tecnologia de Semillas para Centroamerica, Panama y el Caribe.", Seeds Technology Laboratory, Mississippi, 388 pp.

Bunting, A.H and Kuckuck, H., (1970),"Ecological and agronomic studies related to plant exploration.", In: Frankel, O.H. and Bennett, E. (Eds.), (1970), *Genetic Resources in Plants*. IBP Handbook No. 11, Blackwell Sc. Pub., pp. 181-188.

Burke, M.J.; Gusta, L.V.; Quamme, H.A.; Weiser, C. J.; and Li, P.H., (1976),"Freezing and Injury in Plants.", Ann. Rev. Plant Phy. 27:507-528.

Burt, R.L., Pengelly, B.C. and Williams, W.T., (1980),"Network analysis of genetic resources data. III. The elucidation of plant/soil/climate relationships".", Agro-ecosystems 6:119-127.

CIGI, (1982),"Grains & oilseeds. Handling, marketing, processing. (Third Edition)", Canadian International Grains Institute, Winnipeg, Manitoba, 1006 pp.

Cervantes S., T. (Ed.), (1978),"Recursos geneticos disponibles en Mexico.", Sociedad Mexicana de Fitogenetica, Chapingo, Mexico 492 pp.

Chandel, K.P.S., (1981),"Gene pool sampling in field crops.", In: Mehra, K.L. *et al.* (1981), pp. 21-26.

Clark, D.C. and Bass, L.N., (1975),"Effects of storage conditions packaging material, and moisture content on longevity of crimson clover seeds.", Crop Sci. 15:577-580.

CONACYT, (1981),"Guayule; Reencuentro con el desierto." Third Edition, Mexico, 436 pp.

Cooper, C.S. and Qualls, M., (1968),"Seedling vigor evaluation of four Birdsfoot Trefoil varieties grown under two temperature regimes.", Crop Sci. 8:756-757.

Creech, J.L., (1970),"Tactics of exploration and collection.", In: Frankel, O.H. and Bennett, E. (Eds.), (1970), *Genetic Resources in Plants*. IBP Handbook No. 11, Blackwell Sc. Pub., pp. 221-229.

Cromarty, A., (1984),"Techniques for drying seeds.", In: Dickie *et al* (1984).

Cromarty, A.S., Ellis, R.H. and Roberts, E.H., (1985),"The design of seed storage facilities for genetic conservation.", IBPGR Handbooks for genebanks No.1, Roma, 96 pp.

Cruz, A. and Querol L., D., (1985),"Catalogo de la colección de chayote (*Sechium edule*) en el Centro Regional Huatuzco, UACH." Universidad Autónoma Chapingo, Mexico.

Darwin, Charles, (1859),"On the origin of species by means of natural selection.",

Date, R.A. and Halliday, J., (1979),"Colección de cepas de Rhizobium.", In: Mott,... 1979, pp. 23-28.

Davids, M., (1980),"L'evaluation dans la banque de genes; Essai d'application sur une collection de *Phaseolus lunatus L.*", Thesis, Fac. de C. Agron. de l'Etat, Grembloux, Belgique, 195 pp.

Delouche, J.C., (1980),"Preceptos para el almacenamiento de semillas.", Mimeographed. CIAT, Colombia.

Dickie, J.B., Linington, S. and Williams, J.T., (1984),"Seed management techniques for genebanks. Proceedings of a workshop held at the Royal Botanic Gardens, Kew 6-9 July 1983", AGPG: IBPGR/84/68 May 1984, Roma, 294 pp.

Dobzhansky, T.B., (1937),"Genetics and the origin of species.", First Edition, New York.

Duvick, D.N., (1984)."Genetic diversity in major farm crops on the farm and in reserve.", Econ. Bot. 38:161-178.

Ellis, R.H. and Roberts, E.H., (1980a),"Improved equations for the prediction of seed longevity.", Ann. Botany 45:13-30.

Ellis, R.H. and Roberts, E.H., (1980b),"The influence of temperature and moisture on seed viability period in Barley (*Hordeum distichum L.*).", Ann. Botany 45:31-37.

Ellis, R.H., Hong, T.D. and Roberts, E.H., (1985a),"Handbook of seed technology for genebanks. Volume I. Principles and methodology.", IBPGR Handbooks for genebanks. No. 2, Roma.

Ellis, R.H., Hong, T.D. and Roberts, E.H., (1985b),"Handbook of seed technology for genebanks.Vol.II. Compendium of specific germination information and test recommendations", IBPGR Handbook for genebanks. No. 3.

Ellis, R.H., Osei-Bonsu, K. and Roberts, E.H., (1982),"The influence of genotype, temperature and moisture on seed longevity in Chickpea, Cowpea and Soybean.", Ann. Botany 50:69-82.

Esquinas Alcazar, J., (1983),"Los recursos fitogeneticos: una inversión segura para el futuro.", Instituto Nacional de Investigaciones Agrarias, Madrid, Espa´na, 44 pp.

FAO, (1985),"Comisión de Recursos Fitogeneticos. Respuesta de los paises y las instituciones internacionales a la resolución 8/83.", Documents for the first meeting of the Plant Genetic Resources Commission, CPGR/85/3 Add.1, Roma.

FAO, (1987a),"Estudio de las disposiciones juridicas para el posible establecimiento de una red internacional de coleccións base.", GPGR/87/6, Rev. Octubre 87. Plant Genetic Resources Commission, Roma, 38 pp.

FAO, (1987b),"Establecimiento de un fondo internacional para recursos fitogeneticos", G/AGP - 11

FAO, (1987c),"Anuario FAO de produccion 1986", FAO collection: Statistics number 76, Volume 40. FAO Roma.

Fernandez de Oviedo, Gonzalo, (1526),"Sumario de la natural historia de las Indias.", 1979 Edition, Biblioteca Americana, Mexico, 279 pp.

Finlay, K.W. and Konzak, C.F., (1970),"Information storage and retrieval.", In: Frankel, O.H. and Bennett, E. (Eds.), (1970), *Genetic Resources in Plants*. IBP Handbook No. 11, Blackwell Sc. Pub.

Frankel, O.H., (1970),"Genetic conservation in perspective.", In: Frankel, O.H. and Bennett, E. (Eds.), (1970), *Genetic Resources in Plants*. IBP Handbook No. 11, Blackwell Sc. Pub., pp. 469-489.

Frankel, O.H. and Bennett, E. (Eds.), (1970),"*Genetic resources in Plants-Their exploration and conservation.*", IBP Handbook No. 11, Blackwell Scientific Publications, Oxford and Edinburgh, 538 pp.

Gilberth, M.E., (1895),"Dissemination of plants, chiefly by their seeds. A list of illustrative species, collected by Mary E. Gilberth.", Cambridge Botanical Supp. Co., Cambridge, 15 pp.

Goplen, B.P., Cooke, D.A. and Parkings, P., (1972),"Effects of isolation, distance and contamination in sweet clover.", Can. J. Plant Sci. 52:517-524.

Grabe, F., (1970),"Tetrazolium testing handbook for agricultural seeds.", A.O.S.A., 62 pp.

Grant, V., (1963),"El origen de las adaptaciones.", Universidad de Columbia, N.Y., 606 pp.

Grubben, G.J.H., (1977),"Tropical vegetables and their genetic resources.", IBPGR, AGPE/77/23, Roma.

Hanson, J., (1985),"Procedures for handling seeds in genebanks. Practical Manuals for genebanks #1", AGPG: IBPGR /85/86, Roma, 115 pp.

Harlan, J.R., (1951),"Anatomy of gene centers.", Amer. Nat. 85:97-103.

Harlan, J.R., (1971),"Agricultural origins. Centers and non-centers.", Science 174:468-474.

Harlan, J.R., (1975),"Crops and Man.", Amer. Soc. Agron. Madison, Wisconsin, 295 pp.

Harrigton, J.F., (1970),"Seed and pollen storage for conservation of plant gene resources.", In: Frankel, O.H. and Bennett, E. (Ed.), (1970), *Genetic Resources in Plants*. IBP Handbook No. 11, Blackwell Sc. Pub., pp. 501-521.

Hawkes, J.G., (1941),"Potato collecting expeditions in Mexico and South

America.", Bull. Imp. Bur. Pl. Breeding Genetics, Cambridge, 30 pp.

Hawkes, J.G., (1944),"Potato collecting expeditions in Mexico and South America 2. Systematic Classification of the collections.", Bull. Imp. Bur. Pl. Breeding Genetics, Cambridge, 142 pp.

Hawkes, J.G., (1970),"The conservation of short lived asexually propagated plants.", In: Frankel, O.H. and Bennett, E. (Eds.), (1970), Genetic Resources in Plants. IBP Handbook No. 11, Blackwell Sc. Pub., pp. 495-499.

Hawkes, J.G., (1980),"Crop genetic resources: field collection manual.", IBPGR and Eucarpia, 37 pp.

Hernández X., E., (1978),"Exploración etnobotánica para la obtención de plasma germinal para Mexico.", In Cervantes S. T., (1978), Recursos Geneticos disponibles en Mexico. Sociedad Mexicana de Fitogenetica, pp. 3-12.

Heydecker, W. and Coolbear, P., (1977),"Seed treatment for improved performance; Survey and attempted prognosis.", Seed Sci. & Technol. 5:353-425.

Hooker, A.L., (1977),"A plant pathologist's view of germplasm evaluation and utilization.", Crop Sci. 17:689-694.

Howes, G., (1981),"Guidelines for developing descriptor lists.", IBPGR Newsletter 45:26-32.

Huaman, Z., Williams, J.T., Salhuana, W. and Vincent, L., (1977),"Descriptors for the cultivated potato.", IBPGR/77/32, Roma.

IBPGR, (1975),"Annual Report 1975.", AGPE: IBPGR/75/47, FAO, Roma.

IBPGR, (1976a),"Priorities among crops and regions.", AGPE: IBPGR/ 76/8, FAO, Roma.

IBPGR, (1976b),"Report of IBPGR Working group on engineering, design and cost aspects of long-term seed storage facilities.", AGPE: IBPGR/76/25, FAO, Roma, 19 pp.

IBPGR, (1978),"A review of policies and activities (1974-78) and of the prospects for the future.", AGPE: IBPGR/78/24, FAO, Roma.

IBPGR, (1979),"Seed technology for genebanks.", IBPGR Secretariat, Rome, AGP: IBPGR/79/41. Curso del IBPGR.

IBPGR, (1981),"Annual Report 1980.", AGPE: IBPGR/81/24, FAO, Roma.

IBPGR, (1987),"IBPGR Annual Report 1986", IBPGR. ISBN: 92-9043-122-9, Roma,1987

INIPA, (1987),"Documento base para la creación del Programa Nacional de Recursos Geneticos.", Instituto Nacional de Investigación y Promoción Agropecuaria, Lima, Peru, 58 pp.

ISTA, (1966),"International rules for seed testing.", Proc. Int. Seed Test. Ass. 31:1.

James, E., Bass, L.N. and Clark, D.C., (1967a),"Varietal differences in longevity of vegetable seeds and their response to various storage conditions.", Amer. Soc. Hort. 91:521-529.

James, E., Bass, L.N. and Clark, D.C., (1967b),"Effects of variable and constant storage temperatures and subsequent room storage on the viability of certain seeds.", Crop Sci. 7:495-496.

Joshi, B.D., (1981),"Exploration for Amaranth in Northwest India.", IBPGR Newsletter 48:41-50.

Justice, O.L. and Bass, L.N., (1978),"Principles and practices of seed storage", Agriculture Handbook Nro. 506, Washington D.C., 287 pp.

King M.W. and Roberts, E.H., (1979),"The storage of recalcitrant seeds-achievements and possible approaches.", AGP:IBPGR/79/44, Roma, 96 pp.

Leon, J. (Ed.), (1974),"Manual de introduccion de plantas en cultivos tropicales", Food and agriculture Organization, Roma, 138 pp.

Mayer, A.M. and Poljakoff-Mayber, A., (1963),"The germination of seeds.", Pergamon Press, Oxford, 236 pp.

Mehra, K.L., (1981),"Analysis of variation in plant populations.", In: Mehra,K.L. et al. (Ed.), (1981), pp. 14-20.

Mehra, K.L., Arora, R.K. and Wadhim, S.R. (Eds.), (1981),"Plant exploration and collection.", NBPGR Sci. Monogr. No. 3, New Delhi.

MIDINRA, (1984),"Recursos Geneticos, Situacion actual y propuestas.", Ministerio de Agricultura y Reforma Agraria, Managua, Nicaragua, 39 pp., mimeografiado.

Miller, J.F., Hammond, J.J. and Comstock, V.E., (1982),"Diversity analysis and development of a data management information system for the Flax world collection.", Not published.

Monro, H.A.U., (1970),"Manual de fumigacion contra insectos.", FAO, PRONASE, Mexico, 198 pp.

Mooney, P.R., (1980),"Semillas de la tierra. Un recurso publico o privado?", Inter Pares, Ottawa, Canada Development Dialogue. 137 pp.

Mooney, P.R., (1983),"The law of the seed. Another development and plant genetic resources.", Development dialogue 1983 (1-2),172 pp.

Moreno M.,E.; (1976),"Manual para el análisis de semillas", PRONASE, Mexico, 198 p.p.

Mott, G.O., (1979),"Manual for the collection, preservation and characterization of Tropical Forage Resources.", CIAT, Colombia.

Muller, W.H., (1969),"Botany: A functional Approach", The Mac Millan Company, N.Y.

Murata, M.; Roos, E.E; and Tsuchiya, T.; (1977),"Analysis of the first mitotic divisions in germinating seeds.", Barley Genetics Newsl. 7:81-84.

Murata, M., Roos, E.E. and Tsuchiya, T., (1979a),"Relationship between loss of germinability and the occurrence of chromosomal aberrations in artificially aged seeds of barley." Barley Genetics Newsl. 9:65-71.

Murata, M., Roos, E.E. and Tsuchiya, T., (1981),"Chromosome damage induced by artificial seed aging in barley, I. Germinability and frequency of aberrant anaphases at first mitosis." Can. J. Genet. Cytol 23:267-280.

Murata, M., Tsuchiya, T. and Roos, E.E., (1978),"Mitotic chromosomal aberrations in barley induced by accelerated seed aging.", Barley Genetics Newsl. 8:79-82.

Murata, M., Tsuchiya, T. and Roos, E.E., (1979b),"Chromosomal aberrations in plants grown from artificially aged barley seeds.", Amer. Soc. Agron. Abstracts. 71 annual meeting, p. 70.

Murata, M., Tsuchiya, T. and Roos, E.E., (1982),"Chromosome damage induced by artificial seed aging in barley. II. Types of chromosomal aberrations at first mitosis.", Bot. Gaz. 143:111-116.

NAS, (1972),"Genetic vulnerability of major crops.", National Academy of Sciences, Committee on vulnerability of major crops, Washington, D.C.,307 pp.

NAS, (1975),"Underexploited tropical plants with promising economic value.", Washington, 189 pp.

NAS, (1977),"Guayule: An alternative source of natural rubber.", Washington, 80 pp.

NAS, (1979),"Tropical legumes: Resources for the future.", BOSTID publication, National Academy of Sciences, Washington, 331 pp.

Okagami, N. and Kawai, M., (1977),"Dormancy in *Dioscorea*. Giberellin-induced inhibition or promotion in seed germination of *D. tohoro* and *D. tenuipes* in relation to light quality.", Plant Phys. 60:360-366.

Olien, Ch., (1967),"Freezing stress and survival.", Ann. Rev. Plant Phy. 18:387-403.

Plowman, T., (1968),"Folk uses of New World aroids.", Econ. Bot. 23(2):97-122.

Plucknett, D.L., Smith, N.J.H., Williams, J.T. and Murthi,N.A., (1983),"Crop Germplasm Conservation and Developing Countries", Science 220:163-169.

Poehlman,J.M., (1965),"Mejoramiento genetico de las cosechas.",Limusa, Mexico, 453 pp.

Querol L., D., (1982),"Cálculo del tamano de muestra y sistema de manejo de la información para colectas de germoplasma de maiz.", Ponencia en la 10a. Reunión de Maiceros de la Zona Andina, Bolivia. 1982.

Querol L., D., (1983),"Recursos geneticos y derechos de mejorador.", Chapingo 40:57-59.

198GENETIC RESOURCES

Querol, D., (1986),"Report on plant priorities and collections as defined
and executed by the IBPGR over the last 12 years.", IBPGR report,
27 pp. Roma, Managua.

RAFI, (1987),"Vanilla and biotechnology", Bio-communique 1, 5 pp.

Ritchie, Gary A. (Ed.), (1979),"New agricultural crops.", AAAS Selected
Symposium 38, 259 pp.

Roberts, E.H., (1973),"Predicting the storage life of seeds.", Seed Science
and Technology 1:499-514.

Roberts, E.H. and Ellis, R.H., (1977),"Prediction of seed longevity at sub-
zero temperatures and genetic resources conservation.", Nature
(London) 268:431-433.

Roberts, E.H. and King. M.W., (1981),"Problems of storing recalcitrant
seeds during collection and conservation.", Presentation at the
FAO-UNEP-IBPGR Conference, Roma 1981.

Robinson, P.J., Burt, R.L. and Williams, R.T., (1980),"Network analysis of
genetic resources data. II. The use of isozyme data in elucidating
geographical relationships.", Agro-ecosystems 6:111-118.

Roos, E.E., (1977a),"Genetic shifts in stored bean seed.", Bean Improvement Coop. and Nat'l. Dry Bean Council Biennial Conf.
Emeryville, CA. P. 53.

Roos, E.E., (1977b),"Genetic shifts in bean populations during germplasm
preservation.", Ann. Rept. Bean improvement Coop. 20:47-49.

Roos, E.E., (1979a),"Genetic variation within plant introduction lines for
days to flowering.", Ann. Rept. Bean Improvement Coop. 22:80-83.

Roos, E.E., (1979b),"Modeling genetic shifts within mixed bean (*Phaseolus
vulgaris*) populations.", Bean Improvement Coop. and Nat'l. Dry
Bean Council Biennial Conf. Madison, Wis. pp.6-9.

Roos, E.E., (1979c),"Storage behavior of pelleted, tabletted, and taped
Lettuce seed.", J. Amer Soc. Hort. Sci 104:283-288.

Roos, E.E., (1980),"Physiological, biochemical and genetic changes in
seed quality during storage.", Hort. Sci. 15:781-784.

Roos, E.E., (1982),"Induced genetic changes in seed germplasm during
storage.", In: Khan, A.A. (1982) *The physiology and biochemistry of
seed development, dormancy and germination.* Elsevier Biomedical
Press, pp. 409-434.

Roos, E.E., (1984a),"Genetic shifts in mixed bean populations. I. Storage
effects.", Crop Sc. 24:240-244.

Roos, E.E., (1984b),"Genetic shifts in mixed bean populations. II. Effects
of regeneration.", Crop Sc. 24:711-715.

Rubinstein, I., (1979),"The plant seed: development, preservation and
germination.", Academy Press, 1979

Schultes, R.E., (1982),"Plantas alucinógenas", La Prensa Médica Mexicana,
Mexico, 61 pp.

Schultze-Kraft, R., (1979)."Preparación del viaje de colección.", In: Mott,

G.O., (1979), pp. 5-8.

Shafton, A.L., (1979),"Manual de preparación de datos.", IS/GR Publication, 70 pp.

Sinha, G.C., (1981),"Gene pool sampling in tree crops.", In: Mehra, K.L. et al. (Ed.), (1981), pp. 27-33.

Sonoda, R.M., (1979),"Colección y preservación de insectos y organismos patógenos.", In: Mott, G.O., (1979), pp. 29-35.

Stanwood, P.C., (1980),"Tolerance of crop seeds to cooling and storage in liquid nitrogen (-196 C).", Seed Techn. 5:26-31.

Stanwood, P.C. and Bass, L.N., (1981),"Seed germplasm preservation using liquid nitrogen", Seed Sci. & Techn. 9:423-437.

Stanwood, P.C. and Roos, E.E., (1979),"Seed storage of several horticultural species in liquid nitrogen (-196 C).", Hort. Science 14(5):628-630.

Thomas, T.A., (1981),"Gene pool sampling in vegetatively propagated crops.", In: Mehra, K.L. et al. (Ed.), (1981), pp. 34-37.

Thompson, J.R., (1979),"An introduction to seed technology.", J. Wiley and Sons, New York, 252 pp.

Thompson, P.A., (1974),"The use of seed banks for conservation of populations of species and ecotypes.", Biol. Conserv. 6(1):15-19.

Thompson, P.A., (1979a),"The genebank of the Royal Botanic Gardens, Kew and Wakehurst Place.", In: IBPGR, (1979), Seed Technology for Genebanks, IBPGR/79/41, Roma.

Timothy, D.H. and Goodman, M.M., (1979),"Germplasm preservation. The basis of future feast or famine: genetic resources of Maize - An example.", In: Rubenstein, I. (Ed.), (1979), The plant seed: development, preservation and germination. Academic Press.

Tolbert, D.M., Qualset, C.O., Jain, S.C. and Craddoc, J. C.(1979),"A diversity analysis of a world collection of Barley.", Crop Sci. 19:789-794.

UPOV, (1981),"General information", International Union for the Protection of New Varieties of Plants. Ginebra, UPOV Publication 408 (E), Pamphlet.

Vavilov, N.I., (1935),"Phyto-geographic basis of plant breeding.", In: Vavilov, N.I., (1951), Origin, variation, immunity and breeding of cultivated plants. Selected writings. Ronald Press Co., N.Y.

Vavilov, N.I., (1951),"Estudio sobre el origen de las plantas cultivadas.", Spanish version by Felipe Freir. Acme Agency, Buenos Aires, 1962.

Wellhausen, E.J., Roberts, L.M and Hern andez X., E., (1952),"Razas de maiz en Mexico, su origen, caracteristicas y distribución.", Programa de Agricultura Cooperativo, Mexico, 237 pp.

Whitaker, T.W. and Knight Jr., R.J., (1980),"Collecting cultivated and wild cucurbits in Mexico.", Econ. Bot. 34:312-319.

Williams, W.T., Burt,R.L., Pengelly, B.C. and Robins, (1980),"Network

analysis of genetic resources data I. Geographical relationships.",
Agro-ecosystems 6:99-109.

Withers, L.A., (1980),"Tissue culture storage for genetic conservation.",
IBPGR/80/8, FAO, Roma 91 pp.

Withers, L.A., (1981),"Institutes working on tissue culture for genetic
conservation.", IBPGR/81/30, FAO, Roma, 104 pp.

Witt, S.C, (1985),"Biotechnology and genetic diversity.", Briefbook, San
Francisco, California, 145 pp.

Zeven, A.C. and Zeven, N.C., (1976),"Genealogies of 14000 Wheat
varieties.", Wageningen, I.V.P.

Zobel, B., (1970),"Mexican Pines.", In: Frankel, O.H. and Bennett, E.
(Eds.), (1970), *Genetic Resources in Plants*. IBP Handbook No. 11,
Blackwell Sc. Pub., pp. 367-373.

APPENDIX I
Centres of origin of plants with present or potential economic importance in the tropics

This appendix has been ordered alphabetically by groups and by scientific latin name within groups.

The following 18 groups of plants were defined:

Carbohydrates (trees)
Cereals
Dyes
Eddible legumes
Fibers
Forages
Forest trees
Fruits
Industrial
Medicinal
Miscellaneous
Oil sources
Roots and Tubers
Rubber sources
Spices
Stimulants
Sugar
Vegetables

Family	Genera	Species	Common Name	Notes	Centre of Origin
			CARBOHYDRATES (TREES)		
Morac	Artocarpus	altilis Park F	Breadfruit	Fruits & nuts	Polynesia
	Artocarpus	communis		See: A. altilis	
			CEREALS		
Grami	Avena	abysinnica	Oats		Ethiopia
Grami	Hordeum	vulgare	Barley	Seed	Asia
Grami	Oryza	sativa L.	Rice	Seed	China
Grami	Panicum	miliaceum	Millet	Grain	Asia
Grami	Panicum	sonorum?			Mesoamerica
Grami	Sorghum	bicolor	Sorghum	Seed	Abisinia
Grami	Triticale	sp	Triticale	Canada	Canada
Grami	Triticum	aestivum	Wheat	Seed	Asia
Grami	Triticum	vulgare		See: T. aestivum	
Grami	Zea	mays L.	Maize	Seed	Mesoamerica
			DYES		
Morac	Chlorophora	tinctoria	Fustic	Yellow from wood	West Indies
Legum	Haematoxylon	brasiletto	Brasil	Hematoxilin, Blue	South America
Legum	Haematoxylon	campechianum	Logwood	Hematoxilin, Blue	Mesoamerica
Legum	Indigofera	suffruticosa	Indigo		Meso- and S. America
			EDIBLE LEGUMES		
Legum	Cajanus	cajan	Pigeon pea	Human use, fodder	Africa
Legum	Canavalia	ensiformis	Jack Bean	Edible	Mesoamerica

Family	Genus	Species	Common name	Use / Product	Origin
Legum	Cicer	arietinum	Chick-pea	Seed	Africa
Legum	Lablab	niger	Hyacinth bean	Seed	Asia
Legum	Lupinus	mutabilis	Lupin	Seed	Andes
Legum	Phaseolus	acutifolius	Tepary Bean		Mesoamerica
Legum	Phaseolus	anagularis	Adzuki bean	Japan	China
Legum	Phaseolus	calcaratus	Rice Bean	Seed	Asia
Legum	Phaseolus	coccineus	Scarlet Runner Bean		Mesoamerica
Legum	Phaseolus	lunatus	Lima Bean		America
Legum	Phaseolus	mungo	Mung Bean		Asia
Legum	Phaseolus	vulgaris	Common Bean	Seed	Meso- and S. America
Legum	Pisum	sativum	Pea		Mediterranean
Legum	Psophocarpus	tetragonolobus	Winged Bean	Tender pod and roots	Asia
Legum	Vigna	radiata		See: Phaseolus mungo	Asia
Legum	Vigna	Sinensis	Cowpea		Africa
			FIBERS		
Amary	Agave	fourcroydes	Henequen	Ropes, white	Mesoamerica
Amary	Agave	mexicana ?			Mesoamerica
Amary	Agave	sisalana Perr. Sisal		Ropes, yellowish	Mesoamerica
?	Amygdalus ?	communis		Fibers, Fruits	Asia
Grami	Arundo	donax	Cane	Handicraft, baskets	Europe
Urtic	Boehmeria	nivea L. Gaud	Ramie		Asia
Palma	Calamus	spp	Rattan	Stem, Handicraft	Orient, Malaysia
Urtic	Cannabis	sativa	Hemp	Stem	Asia
Legum	Crotalaria	juncea	Kalog-Kalog (Phili.)		India
Ciper	Cyperus	canus Presl.	Sedge	Paper	Pan-tropical
Amary	Furcraea	cabuya	Cabuya	Leaves	Mesoamerica
Malva	Gossypium	arboreum	Cotton		Mesoamerica
Malva	Gossypium	hirsutum	Cotton		Mesoamerica
Malva	Hibiscus	cannabinus L.	Kenaf		Africa
Malva	Hibiscus	sabdariffa	Roselle	Beverages	Africa
Junca	Juncus	glaucus	Handicraft		

Family	Genera	Species	Common Name	Notes	Centre of Origin
Linac	Linum	usitatissimum	Flax	Oil source	Mesoamerica
Cucur	Luffa	cylindrica L.R	Sponge gourd	Sponges	Mesoamerica
Arace	Monstera	deliciosa	Monstera	Handicraft, eddible fruit	Asia
Musac	Musa	textilis Nee	Abaca		Europe
Salic	Salix	viminalis		Leaves	Africa
Lilia	Sansevieria	zeylanica		European rattan	
			FORAGES		
Grami	Cenchrus	ciliaris	Buffel grass	Pasture	Africa
Grami	Chloris	gayana	Rhodes	Grass	Africa
Grami	Cynodon	dactylon	Bermuda	Grass	Pan-tropical
Grami	Cynodon	plectostachyum	Star	Grass	Africa
Grami	Digitaria	decumbens	Pangola	Grass	Africa
Grami	Hyparrhenia	rufa		Jaragua Grass	Africa
Grami	Ixophorus	unisetus		Sweet grass	Mesoamerica
Legum	Leucaena	glauca	Leucaena	Shadow	Mesoamerica
Legum	Leucaena	leucocephala	Ipil Ipil	Vegetable, green pods	
Legum	Lolium	pratense			
Grami	Melinis	minutiflora		Leaves	Africa
Cacta	Opuntia	spp		Panic Grass	
Grami	Panicum	antidotale ?	Blue	Grass	Africa
Grami	Panicum	maximum	Guinea		Tropical America
Grami	Paspalum	notatum	Bahia Grass		
Grami	Pennisetum	purpureum	Elephant, Napier G.		Tropical Africa
Grami	Pennisetum	typhoides	Bulrush Millet	Cereal	West Africa
Grami	Sorghum	bicolor	Sorghum		Africa
Grami	Sorghum	halapense	Johnson Grass	Green manure	Mediterranean
Grami	Sorghum	vulgare		See: S. bicolor	
Grami	Tripsacum	laxum	Guatemala Grass		Mesoamerica
Grami	Zea	mays L.	Maize	Whole plant	Mesoamerica

FOREST

Family	Genus	Species	Common name	Uses	Region
Legum	Acacia	farnesiana	Cassie flower	Timber	Mesoamerica
Legum	Acacia	pennatula		Timber	Mesoamerica
Apoci	Aspidosperma	sp	Quebracho	Timber	America
Morac	Brosimum	alicastrum		Fruit	Mesoamerica
Morac	Brosimum	utile	Cow Tree	Timber	Mesoamerica
Morac	Brosimum	utile?	Cow Tree	Timber	Mesoamerica
Rubia	Calycophyllum	candidissimum		Timber	Mesoamerica
Melia	Carapa	nicaraguense		Timber	Mesoamerica
Legum	Cassia	reticulata		Timber	Mesoamerica
Morac	Cecropia	sp		Timber	Mesoamerica
Melia	Cedrela	odorata ?	Red cedar	Timber	
Bomba	Ceiba	pentandra L. G	Ceiba, Kapok	Fibers, Wood	Africa
Borag	Cordia	alliodora		Timber	Mesoamerica
Borag	Cordia	sp		Timber	Mesoamerica
Eupho	Croton	guatemalensis		Timber	Mesoamerica
Sapin	Cupania	glabra		Timber	Mesoamerica
Legum	Dalbergia	granadillo Sta	Rosewood	Timber	Mesoamerica
	Dalbergia	retusa		See. D. granadillo	
Legum	Enterolobium	cyclocarpum		Timber	Mesoamerica
Bigno	Espatodea	campanulata		Timber	Mesoamerica
Morac	Ficus	petiolaris		Timber	Mesoamerica
Legum	Gliricidia	sepium	Nicarag.	Cocoa shade Wood,	Mesoamerica
Euph?	Hierohyma	alchornevides		Timber	Mesoamerica
Aquif	Ilex	sp		Timber	Mesoamerica
Legum	Inga	paterno?		Timber	Mesoamerica
Melia	Khaya?	nyasica	Mahogany	Timber	Mesoamerica
Rosac	Licania	platypus Hensl		Timber	Mesoamerica
Hamam	Liquidambar	styraciflua	Liquidambar	Timber	Mesoamerica
Tilia	Luehea	sp	Timber		Mesoamerica
Legum	Lysiloma	divaricata		Timber	Mesoamerica
	Melia	azedarach		See: Azadirachta sp.	Mesoamerica
Melas	Miconia	sp		Timber	Mesoamerica

Family	Genera	Species	Common Name	Notes	Centre of Origin
Olac?	Minquartia	guianensis		Timber	Mesoamerica
Eleoc	Muntigia	calabura		Timber	Mesoamerica
Pinac	Pinus	sp	Pine	Timber	Endemic
Legum	Pterocarpus	officinalis		Timber	Mesoamerica
Fagac	Quercus	spp	Oak	74 species in Mexico	Mesoamerica
Legum	Sweetia	sp		Timber	Mesoamerica
Melia	Swietenia	macrophylla	Mahogany		Mesoamerica
Melia	Swietenia	mahogoni	Mahogany	Wood	America
Bigno	Tabebuia	guayacan (hams)		Timber	Mesoamerica
Bigno	Tabebuia	rosea	Pink Pou	Ornamental	Mesoamerica
Combr	Terminalia	amazonia		Timber	Mesoamerica
Combr	Terminalia	chiriquensis		Timber	Mesoamerica
Myris	Virola	hoechnyi		Timber	Mesoamerica
Voqui	Vochysia	sp		Timber	Mesoamerica
Anona	Xylopia	sp		Timber	Mesoamerica
Rutac	Zanthoxylum	microcarpum		Timber	Mesoamerica
Rutac	Zanthoxylum	sp		Timber	Mesoamerica
Flacu	Zuelania	guidonia		Timber	Mesoamerica
			FRUITS		
Cacta	Acanthocereus	pentagonus			Mesoamerica
Brome	Achras	zapota		See: Manilkara achras	Meso- and
	Ananas	comosus L. Mer	Pineapple	Fruit	S. America
Anona	Annona	cherimola	Cherimoya		South America
Anona	Annona	diversifolia	Ilama	Fruit	Mesoamerica
Anona	Annona	muricata L.	Soursop		Tropical America
Anona	Annona	purpurea		Fruit	Mesoamerica
Anona	Annona	reticulata	Custard apple		West-Indies
Anona	Annona	squamosa	Sweetson		Meso- and

Family	Genus	species	Common name	Use	Region
Oxida	Averrhoa	bilimbi	Kamias	Fruit	S. America
Oxida	Averrhoa	carambola L.	Star-fruit	Beverages	Malaysia, Indonesia, Polynesia
Palma	Bactris	gasipaes		See: Guilielma gasipaes	
Malpi	Byrsonima	crassifolia		Timber	Mesoamerica
Sapot	Calocarpum	mammosum	Sapodilla		Meso- and S. America
Caric	Carica	papaya L.	Papaya	Fruit	Mesoamerica
Rutac	Casimiroa	edulis	White Sapote	Fruit	Mesoamerica
Rutac	Casimiroa	sapota			Mesoamerica
Rosac	Chrysobalanus	icaco L.		Fruit	Africa
Cucur	Citrullus	lanatus	Watermelon	Fruit	East Indies
Rutac	Citrus	aurantifolia	Lime	Fruit	Asia
Rutac	Citrus	aurantium	Sour Orange	See: C. sinensis	
Rutac	Citrus	aurantium L.		Fruit	Malaysia
Rutac	Citrus	grandis	Pomelo	See: C. paradisi ?	
Rutac	Citrus	limon	Lemon	Fruit	Asia
Rutac	Citrus	maxima		See: C. paradisi	
Rutac	Citrus	medica L.	Citron	antiemetic, antiseptic	Himalaya
Rutac	Citrus	nobilis		See: C. reticulata	
Rutac	Citrus	paradisi Macf	Grapefruit	Fruit	West Indies
Rutac	Citrus	reticulata	Bla Mandarin	Fruit	China
Rutac	Citrus	sinensis L.	Osb Orange	Fruit	China
Rutac	Citrus	pubescens		Fruit	Asia
Cucur	Cucumis	melo L.	Muskmelon	Fruit	Mesoamerica
Ebena	Diospyros	digyna	Black Sapote	Fruit	Africa
Ebena	Diospyros	ebenaster		Fruit	Mesoamerica
Bomba	Durio	zibethinus	Durian	Fruit	Mesoamerica
Myrta	Eugenia	jambos L.	Rose Apple	Fruit	Malaysia
Rosac	Fragaria	spp	Strawberry		India
Guiti	Garcinia	mangostana	Mangosteen	Aril	Malaysia
Palma	Guilielma	gasipaes	Peach	Palm	America

Family	Genera	Species	Common Name	Notes	Centre of Origin
Legum	Hymenaea	courbaril L.	Locust Tree	Copal	Mesoamerica
Legum	Inga	spp		Fruit	America
Sapin	Litchi	chinensis Sonn	Litchi	Eddible aril	China
Sapot	Lucuma	mammosa	Egg Fruit	L. nervosa?	America
Rosac	Malus	comunis	Apple	Fruit	
Rosac	Malus	pumila Mill.	Apple		
Gutif	Mammea	americana	Mamey apple		South America
Anaca	Mangifera	indica L.	Mango		India
Sapot	Manilkara	achras Mill.Fo	Sapodilla	See: M. achras	Mesoamerica
Sapot	Manilkara	zapodilla			
Musac	Musa	balbisiana	Banana	Fruit	Asia
Musac	Musa	paradisiaca	Plantain	Fruit	Asia
Sapin	Nephelium	lappaceum	Rambutan	Eddible aril	Malaysia
Cacta	Opuntia	ficus-indica			
Cacta	Opuntia	spp			
Bigno	Parmentiera		Cuachilote	Fruit	Mesoamerica
Passi	Passiflora	edulis	Passion fruit	Fruit	Mesoamerica
Passi	Passiflora	edulis Sims	Juss Sweet Granadilla	Fruit	South America
Passi	Passiflora	ligularis	Passion fruit	Fruit	America
Passi	Passiflora	quadrangularis		Fruit	South America
Laura	Persea	americana Mill	Avocado	Fruit	Mesoamerica
Laura	Persea	schiedeana	Avocado	Fruit	Mesoamerica
Palma	Phoenix	dactylifera	Date	Palm	Middle East
Eupho	Phyllanthus	acidus L.Skeel	Otaheite Gooseberry	Fruit	Asia
	Pouteria	campechiania		See: Lucuma nervosa	
Rosac	Prunus	armeniaca L.	Apricot	Fruit	Mesoamerica
Rosac	Prunus	avium L.	Cherry		Asia
Rosac	Prunus	capuli			China
Rosac	Prunus	domestica L.	Plum		Mesoamerica
Rosac	Prunus	persica	Peach		Asia
Myrta	Psidium	guajava L.	Guava	Fruit	Mesoamerica
Punic	Punica	granatum l	Pomegranate	Fruit	Asia

Family	Genus	species	Common name	Use	Origin
Rosac	Pyrus	communis L.	Pear	Fruit	Mesoamerica
Rosac	Rubus	spp		Fruit	Mesoamerica
Anaca	Spondias	mombin L.	Mombin	Fruit	India
Anaca	Spondias	purpurea L.	Mombin	Fruit	India
	Syzygium	jambos		See: Eugenia jambos	Gulf of Bengal
Legum	Tamarindus	indica L.	Tamarind	Fruit	
Combr	Terminalia	catappa	Tanin, Oil		
Vitac	Vitis	vinifera L.	Grapes		
INDUSTRIAL					
Cheno	Beta	vulgaris	Beet	Fruit	Mediterranean
Caesa	Caesalpinia	coriaria	Divi-Divi	Fruit	Mesoamerica
Bigno	Crescentia	cujete	Calabash		Mesoamerica
Buxac	Simondsia	chinensis	Jojoba	Oil	Mesoamerica
MEDICINAL					
Amary	Aloe	spicata	Aloe	Acibar, bacteriostatic	Africa
Arist	Aristolochia	sp	Antiviper	Mesoamerica	Asia
Urtic	Cannabis	sativa var.	Marihuana	var. indica	America
Apocy	Catharanthus	roseus	Periwinckle	Ornamental	Mesoamerica
Rubia	Cephaelis	ipecacuanha	Ipecac	Emetine, Cefeline	South America
Rubia	Cinchona	succirubra	Cinchona, Quinine	C. calysaya, various sp.	China
Laura	Cinnamomum	camphora	Camphor	Resin,industrial,synthet.	Mesoamerica
Solan	Datura	stramonium	Datura	Daturin, hypnotic	Mesoamerica
Diosc	Dioscorea	composita	Wild Yam	Oestrogens	South America
Erytr	Erythroxylum	coca L.	Coca	Cocaine	Mesoamerica
Convo	Exogonium	purga	Jalap	Purgative	
Eupho	Hippomane	mancinella			Mesoamerica
	Ipomoea	purga		See: Exogonium purga	
Cacta	Lophophora	williamsii	Peyotl	Alucinogen	Mesoamerica
Labia	Melissa	officinalis		Infusion	Orient
Solan	Nicotiana	rustica	Tobacco (wild)	Leaves	Mesoamerica
Simar	Quassia	amara	Quassia	Insecticide	Mesoamerica

Family	Genera	Species	Common Name	Notes	Centre of Origin
Labia	Rosmarinus	officinalis	Rosemarie	Dry climate	Europe
Labia	Salvia	hispanica	Spice		Mesoamerica
Logan	Strychnos	nux-vomica	Nux vomica		Asia
Apoci	Thevetia	plumeriaefolia			Mesoamerica
			MISCELLANEOUS		
Palma	Areca	catechu	Betel nut	Masticatory	Asia
Grami	Arundinaria	spp	Bamboo	Construtions	China
Legum	Astragalus	mollissimus	Tragacanth	Glue/Pharmacy	Endemic
Grami	Bambusa	vulgaris	Bamboo	Food, construction	Asia
Compo	Chrysanthemum	cinerariaefoli	Pyrethrum	Pyretrins (riaefolium)	Dalmatia
Palma	Copernicia	cerifera	Carnauba palm	Wax, oil	America
Legum	Crotalaria	sp	Crotulosia	Green manure	Pan-tropical
Compo	Dahlia	rosea	Dahlia	Ornamental	Mesoamerica
	Dolichos	lablab		See: Lablab niger	
Cucur	Lagenaria	siceraria Moli	Bottle gourd	Fruit	Meso- and S. America
Cacta	Lemaireocereu	spp.		Live fences	Mesoamerica
Legum	Myroxylon	balsamun	Balsam of Tolu	Drug	South America
Cacta	Nopalea	cochinellifera	Cochineal	cactus	Mesoamerica
Sapin	Paullinia	cupana	Guarana	Beverages	South America
Palma	Phytelephas	macrocarpa	Ivory-nut	Palm	America
Legum	Pueraria	javanica?	Kudzu	Green cover	Asia
Rhizo	Rhizophora	mangle	Mangrove	Bark, tanning, wood	Mesoamerica
Palma	Sabal	mexicana		Handicraft, roofs	
			OIL SOURCES		
Legum	Arachis	hipogea L.	Peanuts	Seed	South America
Lecit	Bertholletia	excelsa Berg	Brazil nut	Lecitidiacea, Nuts	South America
Cruci	Brassica	campestris	Rape seed	Seed	India
Compo	Carthamus	tinctorius	Safflower	Oil dye	Africa

Family	Genus	Species	Common name	Note	Region
Palma	Cocos	nucifera	Coconut palm	Var. nana	Malaysia
Palma	Cocos	nucifera L.	Coconut palm	Fruit	Polynesia
Bigno	Crescentia	alata H.B.K.		Fruit	Mesoamerica
Palma	Elaeis	guineensis	African Oil Palm	Fruit	Africa
Palma	Elaeis	oleifera H.B.K	American Oil Palm	Fruit	South America
Legum	Glycine	max L. Merr	Soyabean	Seed	Eastern Asia
Compo	Helianthus	annuus L.	Sunflower	Seed	Mesoamerica
Prote	Macadamia	ternifolia	Macadamia	Eddible nut	Australia
Moran	Moringa	oleifera	Horse-radish tree	Spice, root	India
Oleac	Olea	europea	Olive	Fruit	Caucasus
Rosac	Prunus	amygdalus	Almonds	Nut	
Eupho	Ricinus	communis L.	Castor-oil plant	Seed	Africa
Pedal	Sesamum	indicum L.	Sesame	Seed	Africa
	Sesamun	orientale		See: S. indicum	

ROOTS AND TUBERS

Family	Genus	Species	Common name	Note	Region
Amary	Bomarea	edulis			Mesoamerica
Canna	Canna	edulis	Canna	Edible rhizome	Mesoamerica
Arace	Colocasia	esculenta L.	Dasheen, Taro		Asia
Diosc	Dioscorea	alata	White Yam		Asia
Diosc	Dioscorea	cayenensis	Yellow Yam		Asia
Compo	Helianthus	tuberosus	Jerusalem Artichoke	Contains Inuline	America
Convo	Ipomoea	batatas L.Poir	Sweet potato		Mesoamerica
Eupho	Manihot	esculenta	Cassava		America
Maran	Maranta	arundinacea	Arrowroot	Starch	Mesoamerica
Oxali	Oxalis	tuberosa	Oca		Andes
Legum	Pachyrrhizus	erosus L.Urban	Yam bean		Mesoamerica
Solan	Solanum	tuberosum L.	otato	Raw root	South America
Tropa	Tropaealum	tuberosum	Anu		Andes
Basel	Ullucus	tuberosus	Ullucu		Andes
Arace	Xanthosoma	sagittifolium	Tania		Mesoamerica

Family	Genera	Species	Common Name	Notes	Centre of Origin
			RUBBER		
Morac	Castilla	elastica Cerv.	Castilloa Rubber	Resin	Mesoamerica
Morac	Ficus	elastica Roxb.	Indian Rubber tree	Sap	Asia
Eupho	Manihot	dichotoma	Jequie-Manicoba rubb		Brazil
Eupho	Manihot	glaziovii Muel	Ceara-rubber	Resin	Brazil
	Manilkara	zapota		See: M. Achras	
Compo	Parthenium	argentatum A.G	Guayule	Whole plant	Mexico
			SPICES		
Cruci	Brassica	alba	White mustard	Seed	Mediterranean
Cruci	Brassica	nigra	Black Mustard	Seed	Eurasia
Solan	Capsicum	frutescens var	Tree chili pepper	Fruit	Mesoamerica
Umbel	Carum	carvi	Caraway		Eurasia
Laura	Cinnamomum	zeylanicum	Cinnamon	Bark	India
Umbel	Coriandrum	sativum	Coriander	Leaves	Mediterranean
Zingi	Curcuma	domestica	Turmeric	Root	India
	Curcuma	longa		See: C. domestica	
Zyngi	Elettaria	cardamomum	Cardamom	Seed	India
Umbel	Eryngium	foetium			
	Eugenia	aromatica		See: Syzygium aromaticum	
Umbel	Foeniculum	vulgare	Fennel	Seed	Mediterranean
Labia	Hyssopus	officinalis	Leaves		Midle Orient
Verbe	Lippia	micromeria	Spanish Thyme	Substitute european thym	South America
Labia	Majorana	hortensis	Marjoram		Europe
Labia	Mentha	spicata	Mint	Leaves	Europe
	Mentha	viridis		See: M. spicata	
Labia	Mentha	x piperita	Mint	Essencial oils	Temperate reg.
Labia	Myristica	fragrans	Nutmeg	Seed	Moluccas
Labia	Ocimum	basilicum	Sweet Basil	Leaves	India

Family	Genus	species	Common name	Part/Use	Origin
Labia	Origanum	majorana	Marjoram		Europe
Labia	Origanum	vulgare	Oregano		Mediterranean
Umbel	Petroselinum	crispum	Parsley	See: P.crispum	
Umbel	Petroselinum	sativum		Seed	Mesoamerica
Myrta	Pimenta	dioica	Anise	Seed	Mediterranean
Umbel	Pimpinella	anisum	Black pepper	Seed	India
Piper	Piper	nigrum	Clove	Buds= cloves	Moluccas
Myrta	Syzygium	aromaticum	Thyme	Leaf; medicinal	Mediterranean
Labia	Thymus	vulgaris	Vanilla	Vainillin	Mesoamerica
Orqui	Vanilla	fragrans		See: V. fragrans	
	Vanilla	planifolia	Ginger	Root	Asia
Zingi	Zingiber	officinale			

STIMULANTS

Family	Genus	species	Common name	Part/Use	Origin
Amary	Agave	atrovirens	Spanish: Maguey	Paper,Ropes,Leaves, pulque	Mesoamerica
Amary	Agave	tequilana	Agave	Roots :tequila	Mesoamerica
Theac	Camellia	sinensis L.	Tea	Infusion	Burma
Rubia	Coffea	arabica L.	Coffee	Seed	Ethiopia
Rubia	Coffea	canephora	Pie Robusta		Africa
Rubia	Coffea	liberica Hiero	Liberian Coffee		Liberia
Sterc	Cola	acuminata Bean	Kola	Seed	Africa
Solan	Nicotiana	tabacum L.	Tobacco	Leaves	Mesoamerica
Sterc	Theobroma	cacao L.	Cacao	Seed	Mesoamerica

SUGAR

Family	Genus	species	Common name	Part/Use	Origin
Grami	Saccharum	officinarum L.	Sugarcane	Cane	Asia
Grami	Sorghum	vulgare var.	Sweet Sorghum	Var. saccharatum?	Africa

VEGETABLES

Family	Genus	species	Common name	Part/Use	Origin
Lilia	Abelmoschus	esculentus		See: Hibiscus esculentus	
	Allium	cepa L.	Onion	Whole plant	China
	Allium	porrum L.		See: A. ampeloprasum	

Family	Genera	Species	Common Name	Notes	Centre of Origin
Lilia	Allium	sativum L.	Garlic	Whole plant	Mediterranean
Umbel	Apium	graveolens L.	Celery	Whole plant	Mediterranean
Lilia	Asparagus	officinalis L.	Asparagus		Europe
Cheno	Beta	vulgaris	Beet		Mediterranean
Basel	Blasella	alba L.	Malabar nightshade	Indian spinach, Leaves	Asia
Cruci	Brassica	oleracea var.	Broccoli	Var. italica	Eurasia
Cruci	Brassica	oleracea var.	Cauliflower	Var. botrytis	Eurasia
Cruci	Brassica	oleracea var.	Cabbage	Var. capitata	Eurasia
Cruci	Brassica	rapa	Turnip	Root	Europe
Solan	Capsicum	annuum	Chili Pepper	Fruit	Mesoamerica
	Citrullus	vulgaris		See: C. lanatus	Africa
Cucur	Cucumis	sativus L.	Cucumber	Fruit	Indochina-India
Cucur	Cucurbita	mixta	Squash	Fruit	Mesoamerica
Cucur	Cucurbita	moschata Duch.	Pumpkin	Fruit	Mesoamerica
Cucur	Cucurbita	pepo L.	Field Pumpkin	Fruit	Mesoamerica
Umbel	Daucus	carota	Carrots	Root	Eurasia
Malva	Hibiscus	esculentus	Okra		Africa
Compo	Lactuca	sativa	Lettuce	Leaves	Eurasia
Solan	Lycopersicum	esculentum	Tomato	Fruit	Mesoamerica
Cruci	Nasturtium	officinale	Watercress	Leaves	Eurasia
Solan	Physalis	xocarpa		Fruit	Mesoamerica
Cruci	Raphanus	sativus	Radish	Root, salads	Asia
Cucur	Sechium	edule	Christophine	Chayote Fruit	Mesoamerica
Solan	Solanum	melongena	Eggplant	Fruit	India
Solan	Solanum	muricatum	Papino	Fruit	Andes
Cheno	Spinacea	oleracea L.	Spinach	Leaves	Asia
Legum	Vigna	unguiculata	Stringbean	Immature pods	Africa

Appendix II

Manual for the use of a Collecting sheet

Introduction

This manual should be used to correctly fill in the collecting sheet, which is the main document for any gene bank.
Its utilization is recommended to be able to systematize the information obtained by different people, at different times and with different species.

In the case of a collecting sheet, there are 11 information categories:

0.   General Information
I.   Taxonomy
II.   Geography
III. Ecology
IV.   Characteristics of the material
V.   The Informant
VI.   The crop
VII. Utilization
VIII. The Collection
IX.   Associated collections
X.   Supplemental information

Each one of these categories organizes the information obtained in the field.

The user of the collecting sheet should introduce the number which corresponds to the descriptor state in the square beside the descriptor.

Data will be transferred from the sheet into a computer. Therefore the following rules should be observed:

1.   Use capital letters from A to Z, arabic numerals from 0
      to 9 and if necessary the symbols - / ( ) * , . and blank
      spaces.
2.   Write with a pencil, as the ink may disappear after a few
      years.
3.   If the information is not available, just leave blank spaces.

It should be remembered that some of the data may not
be of interest to the collector but may be important for another
user of the genebank.
    In the lower part of the sheet you will find tree detach-
able pieces of cardboard, each with the same sheet number
printed in red, and with space to write the collection name
according to the collectors taste.
    These cardboard pieces should be used as follows:
    One will go inside the bag with the sample, the second
one will be stapled outside of the bag and the third may be
used for the herbarium specimen.

Use of the descriptors

0) GENERAL INFORMATION

Date of collection: It should be written as year, month, day for
the sorting in the computer.
E.g. September 23 1990 is 900923
Accession number: This information will be filled out by the
curator in the genebank and should not be filled by the collector.
Sheet number: This is a unique number and can not be
changed by the collector. It is thought to avoid confusions by
duplicate numbering of different collections. The same number
is also printed in the bottom of the sheet.
Names of the collection: Whatever name the collector wants to
give to the sample. This data is not used by the genebank.

I. TAXONOMY

The data on **Family, genus, species, subspecies** and **variety** should be written in full on the line besides the descriptor. The squares will be filled in the following way:

FAMILY   : First five letters
GENUS   : First ten letters
SPECIES   : First five letters
SUBSPECIES : First five letters
VARIETY   : Should be an abbreviation of the name as
                      proposed by Briggle et al. (1960) with 4 letters.

Common name and local name: Should be filled out so as to insure they fit in the 12 available spaces.

E.g.   Common name   **MAIZE**
          Local name   **YELLOW**

II. GEOGRAPHY

Place of collection: 15 spaces available.
Municipality of collection: Should be written on the line, codes will be introduced in the genebank.
State of collection : Same as above
Country of collection: Use the official FAO three letter codes, included at the end of this guide.
Latitude: Will be transformed into Degrees and hundredths of degree.
Minutes can be transformed into hundredths of degrees by multiplying by 1.66
E.g. 17 degrees 30' is written as 17.50
Longitude: Same as Latitude
E.g. 65 degrees 44' is written as 65.73
Altitude: In meters above sea level.

All data for the following items should be introduced in the boxes besides the descriptors.

III. ECOLOGY

15) Physiography

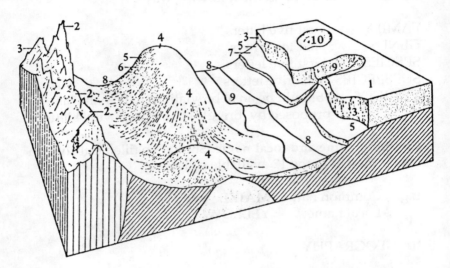

		6.	Medium slope
1.	Level	7.	Terrace
2.	Top of mountain	8.	Light slope
3.	Steep slope	9	Open depression
4.	Rounded top	10.	Closed depression
5.	Strong slope	11.	Other

16) Description of the site
1. Field: cultivated field, with any type of crop.
2. Roadside: Border of any land communication way.
3. Sweet water shore: River, lake or lagoon shore.
4. Swamp: sweet water saturated soil.
5. Sea shore: salt water shore.
6. Desert: arid area without significant vegetation.
7. Pasture land: area cultivated with forages or used as grazing area.
8. Wood: transition area from temperate to warm climate.

9.   Evergreen wood: temperate area.
10   Low tropical forest: tropical area with primary vegeta-
       tion growing less than 3 m in height.
11.   Medium tropical forest: tropical area with primary
       vegetation growing less than 15 m in height.
12.   High tropical forest: tropical area with primary vegeta-
       tion growing above 15 m in height.
13.   Garden: Area close to a house, not necessarily culti-
       vated.
14.   Family garden: Small cultivated area, with diverse
       species of various uses.
15.   Other: any case not included in the previous items.

17) Type of soil
Please write the main type of soil (a) and the secondary type
(b), using one number from the following.
1.   Sandy
2.   Lime
3.   Clay
4.   Organic
5.   Stony
6.   Other: any case not included in the previous items.

18) Shadiness
This refers specifically to the collected plant and not to the
general shading of the area.
1.   Sunny: the plant grows without cover.
2.   Partly shaded: the plant grows under other plants.
3.   Shaded: the plant grows under a dense vegetation.
4.   Other: any case not included in the previous items.

IV. CHARACTERISTICS OF THE MATERIAL

19) Growth conditions
1.   Wild: no human intervention
2.   Tolerated: plant is neither encouraged nor cultivated.
       It is not considered a weed or has some known use in
       the community.

3.   Encouraged: plant which is not planted but nurtured in order to obtain something from it.
4.   Cultivated: plant which is kept by the peasant during the whole growth cycle.

20)   Growth Habit
1.   Crawling: plant which does not grow beyond 10 cm above its rooting surface.
2.   Herbaceous: plant of up to 30 cm in height, and in the case of grasses up to 4 m.
3.   Bushy: plant without a central trunk, branched, independently of its height.
4.   Tree: plant with a central trunk and a canopy.
5.   Epiphytic: plant growing on other plants.
6.   Water growing: plant growing under water or on the water, without direct contact with dry soil.
7.   Climbing: plant hanging from trees.
8.   Other: any case not included in the previous items.

21) Abundance
One may find from a very low frequency of plants in isolated patches all the way into dense monocrop cultivated fields.
1.   Very scarce: isolated plant. No other plants of the same species are found.
2.   Scarce.
3.   Not very frequent: more than 3 plants of the same size and other species, for each plant of the collected species.
4.   Frequent.
5.   Very frequent: more than 3 plants of the collected species for each plant of the same size and other species.
6.   Solid population: rare occurrence of plants of other species.

22) Variability of the population
This information is important, as it will allow to decide whether one or many collections must be made.
In the case 1 and 2 (Homogeneous and little variability), a sample of the biggest number of plants (up to 200) will be taken and bulked to make up the collection.

In the cases 3,4 and 5 (Heterogeneous, very heterogeneous and if it could not be determined), two types of collections will be made:

1.   One collection for each group of similar plants. There will be as many collections as there are distinct types of plants (biased sample).
2.   One collection in which all the available plant types will be bulked, trying to maintain the proportion of the available phenotypes (random sample).

23)   Biological Cycle
1.   Spring annual: plant which starts its growth during spring.
2.   Intermediate annual: plant which starts its growth before spring.
3.   Winter annual: plant which starts its growth in autumn, passes the winter and flowers in spring or summer.
4.   Biannual: plant with vegetative growth during the first year and which produces seeds the second.
5.   Short-lived Perennial : 2 - 5 years.
6.   Medium-lived Perennial : 6 to 15 years.
7.   Long-lived Perennial : 16 to 50 years.
8.   Very long lived Perennial : over 50 years.
9.   Unknown.

24)   Reproductive Mechanism
1.   Asexual (Vegetative): no seeds produced or seeds non viable.
2.   Through seed: only reproduces through seed under natural conditions.
3.   Both.

25)   Type of Material
1.   Native species in wild state: all species which originate in the country or area of collection not under cultivation.
2.   Native variety: same as above, but under cultivation.
3.   Special non-cultivated material: all material worked on by breeders but not commercially available.
4.   Modern bred variety: native or introduced species which

has passed a modern breeding process.
5.   Other variety (introduced, obsolete, etc.): any other
        variety not included in the aforementioned categories
        and is found under cultivation.
6.   Unknown.

V.   THE INFORMANT

26)   Name of the informant
Try to record both family names.

27)   Activity
1.   Peasant: any person who has agriculture as a main
        source of income.
2.   Biologist.
3.   Breeder, agricultural engineer.
4.   Medicine man, witch doctor.
5.   Doctor.
6.   Inhabitant: anyone who lives in the area.

28)   Characteristics
1.   Not a peasant.
2.   Small peasant: person cultivating less than 5 Ha.
3.   Medium peasant: person cultivating between 5 and 10
        Ha.
4.   Farmer or landlord: person owning over 10 Ha.

29)   Land Property
1.   Collective Property.
2.   Individual Property.
3.   Rented land.
4.   Others: any case not included in the previous items.

30)   Relationship Between Production and the Market
The question is related to the whole of the produce from the
farm and its destination.
1.   Consumed (direct use).
2.   Mixed.

3.   100% commercial.

VI. THE CROP
These points will only be filled in the case of cultivated material.

31)   Planting date: Year.month.date written as YY.MM.DD.
32)   Harvest date: Year.month.date written as YY.MM.DD.
33)   Second planting date: Year.month.date written as YY.MM.DD.
34)   Second harvest date: Year.month.date written as YY.MM.DD.
35)   Amount of seeds used: in kg per hectare.
36)   Yield: in kg per hectare.
37)   Relationship Between Production and the Market
This is similar to point 30), but it only refers to the crop being collected, and not to all crops planted by the peasant.
1.   Consumed (direct use).
2.   Mixed.
3.   100% commercial.

VII. UTILIZATION

In the case of points 38 and 39, the uses and the parts of the plant used should be described. The possible uses are:
1.   Food source
2.   Medicinal: including local medicinal practices.
3.   Industrial: including local industrial use.
4.   Fodder crop
5.   Ornamental
6.   Ceremonial
7.   Weed
8.   None
9.   Other: any case not included in the previous items.

The parts of the plant used are:
1.   Seed
2.   Flower
3.   Fruit

4.   Stem
5.   Leave
6.   Root
7.   Tuber
8.   Bark
9.   The whole plant
10.   None
11.   Other: any case not included in the previous items.

Example of data 38 and 39:
A maize collection is made. The main use is 1 (Food source) and
the part of the plant used for food is 1 (Seed). The secondary
use could be 4 (Fodder crop) and the part of the plant could be
9 (the whole plant).

40) Specific use and way of use
If further information is needed, it should be written here. For
example, in the case of medicinal plants, doses and way of
administration should be specified.

VIII. THE COLLECTION

41)   Type of collected material
This information will define the type of processing and storage
needed.
1.   Seed.
2.   Fruit.
3.   Plants.
4.   Cutting.
5.   Other: any case not included in the previous items.

42)   Type of Collection
1.   Field: material just harvested.
2.   Market: this implies more difficulties in the identifica-
       tion of the material and its source.
3.   Seeds store: may imply a mixture of genotypes.
4.   Peasant's store: may be a store or just the house.
5.   Other: any case not included in the previous items.

43)   Age of the sample
The number of months since seeds were harvested helps to establish whether regeneration is necessary.

44)   Sampling method
1.   Random: the best way to take a sample.
2.   Best according to the informant: biased sample.
3.   Best according to the collector: biased sample.
4.   Worst according to the informant: leftover seeds or grains.
5.   Worst according to the collector: leftover seeds or grains.
6.   Other: any case not included in the previous items.

45)   Amount collected
The amount is a figure and the units are:
1.   Seeds
2.   Grains
3.   Fruits
4.   Plants
5.   Spikes
6.   Tubers
7.   Ears
8.   Cuttings
9.   Grams
10.   Kilograms
11.   Measures
12.   Other: any case not included in the previous items.

Example: 500 grams: amount= 500 unit = 9.

46)   Herbarium specimen
Whether a specimen was taken or not.

47)   Photograph
Whether a photograph was taken or not. If one was taken, indicate the number of roll and the number of shot.

IX.   ASSOCIATED COLLECTIONS

This will allow to maintain a control over ecosystems, multiple collections due to variability and mixed cropping systems.

The sheet numbers will be filled in by the collector and the accession numbers by the curator in the Genebank. The possible types of association are:
1.   Multiple samples due to heterogeneity
2.   Main crop
3.   Crop associated to this collection
4.   Weed of this collection
5.   Ecosystem
6.   Other

Example: A maize field, intercropped with beans, with abundant pigweed of an aggressive kind. The maize crop has evident variability. (See included collecting sheet).

The collecting sheet being worked on is number 1338.

Collecting sheet number 1339 would have 3 as type of association and would be the beans sample.

Collecting sheet number 1340 would have 4 as type of association and would be the pigweed sample.

Collecting sheet number 1341 would have 1 as type of association and would be the biased maize sample, from the general sample in sheet 1339.

X.   SUPPLEMENTAL INFORMATION

52)   Notes (29 spaces)

All further information which should be coded for its introduction to the computer.

53)   Name of the collector (12 spaces)

54)   Name of the taxonomic identifier (12 spaces)

Notes: This will not be recorded in the computer, but will be

read by the curator in the genebank. It may include information as disease occurrence or pests observed.

REFERENCES

BRIGGLE, L. W.; SCHMIDT, J. W.; HEYNE, E. G. and YOUNG, H.
C. (1960)
    Rules for abbreviating wheat variety names. Agr. J. 52-61.

COLLECTING SHEETS USED AS BACKGROUND

CIAT, Colombia (Bean collecting sheet).
INIA, Mexico (Germplasm collecting sheet).
Plant Gene Resources of Canada, Canada. Plant Genetic Resources
    Expedition Collection Record Sheet.
Ortega P., R. and Hernandez X., E. Ideas sobre variation,
    coleccion y documentacion de cultivares nativos.
Matsuo, T. ed. JIBP Synthesis. Vol 5. Gene conservation, exploration,
    collection, preservation and utilization of genetic resources.
    Tokyo, University of Tokyo Press, p. 18.

Date of collection `9 0 0 3 2 3`
Y Y M M D D

Accession number `⬚⬚⬚⬚⬚⬚`

Sheet number `1338`

Genetic Resources Collecting Sheet

Name of the collection _____

I. Taxonomy

Family _____ `G R A M I`

Genus _____ `Z E A`

Species _____ `M A Y S`

Subspecies _____

Variety _____

Common name `M A I Z E`

Local name `Y E L L O W`

II. Geography

Place of collection `T E P A L C I N G O`

Municipality of collection _____ `1 8 3 5`

State of collection `G U E R R E R O` `1 6`

Country of collection _____ `M E X`

Latitude _____ `1 7 . 5 0`

Longitude _____ `6 5 . 7 3`

Altitude (metres a. sea) _____ `1 4 0 0`

III. Ecology

15) Physiography `1`

1. Level
2. Top of mountain
3. Steep slope
4. Rounded top
5. Strong slope
6. Medium slope
7. Terrace
8. Light slope
9 Open depression
10. Closed depression
11. Other

16) Description of the site `1`

1. Field
2. Roadside
3. Freshwater shore
4. Swamp
5. Seashore
6. Desert
7. Pasture land
8. Wood
9. Evergreen wood
10. Low tropical forest
11. Medium tropical forest
12. High tropical fores t
13. Garden
14. Family garden
15. Other

17) Type of soil `1` `2`

1. Sandy
2. Lime
3. Clay
4. Organic
5. Stony
6. Other

18) Shadiness `1`

1. Sunny
2. Partly shaded
3. Shaded
4. Other

IV. Characteristics of the material

19) Growth conditions `4`

1. Wild
2. Tolerated
3. Encouraged
4. Cultivated

20) Growth Habit `2`

1. Crawling
2. Herbaceous
3. Bushy
4. Tree
5. Epiphitic
6. Water growing
7. Climbing
8. Other

21) Abundancy `5`

1. Very scarce
2. Scarce
3. Not very frequent
4. Frequent
5. Very frequent
6. Solid population

22) Variability of the population `⬚`

1. Homogeneous
   (100% uniform)
2. Little variability
   (variability is not very visible)
3. Heterogenous
4. Very heterogenous
5. Could not be determined
Note:In cases 3, 4 and 5
various samples should be taken

23) Biological Cycle `1`

1. Spring annual
2. Intermediate annual
3. Winter annual
4. Biannual
5. Short-lived Perennial (2 - 5 years)
6. Medium-lived Perennial (6 to 15 years)
7. Long-lived Perennial (16 to 50 years)
8. Very long lived Perennial (over 50 years)
9. Unknown

24) Reproductive Mechanism `2`

1. Asexual (Vegetative)
2. Through seed
3. Both

25) Type of Material `2`

1. Native species in wild state
2. Native variety
3. Special non-cultivated material
4. Modern bred variety
5. Other variety (introduced, obsolete, etc.)
6. Unknown

Sheet Number 1338	Sheet Number 1338	Sheet Number 1338
Name of the collection ____	Name of the collection ____	Name of the collection ____

V. The Informant

26) Name `J U A N   M A T O S`

27) Activity `1`
1. Peasant
2. Biologist
3. Breeder, agricultural engineer
4. Medicine man, witch doctor
5. Doctor
6. Inhabitant

28) Characteristics `2`
1. Not a peasant
2. Small peasant
3. Medium peasant
4. Farmer or landlord

29) Land Property `2`
1. Collective Property
2. Individual Property
3. Rented land
4. Others

30) Relationship Between Production and the Market `2`
1. Consumed (direct use)
2. Mixed
3. 100% commercial

VI. The Crop

31) Planting date

32) Harvest date

33) Second planting date

34) Second harvest date

Y Y M M D D

35) Amount of seed used (kg. per hectare)

36) Yield (kg. per hectare) `1 0 0 0`

37) Relationship Between Production and the Market `2`
1. Consumed (direct use)
2. Mixed
3. 100% commercial

VII. Utilisation

38) Main use `1` Part of the plant `1`

39) Secondary use `4` Part of the Plant `9`

40) Specific use and way of use

Uses
1. Food source
2. Medicinal
3. Industrial
4. Fodder crop
5. Ornamental
6. Ceremonial
7. Weed
8. None
9. Others

Parts of the Plant
1. Seed
2. Flower
3. Fruit
4. Stem
5. Leaf
6. Root
7. Tuber
8. Bark
9. The whole plant
10. None
11. Other

VIII. The Collection

41) Type of collected material `1`
1. Seed   4. Cutting
2. Fruit   5. Other
3. Plants

44) Sampling method `1`
1. Random
2. Best according to the informant
3. Best according to the collector
4. Worst according to the informant
5. Worst according to the collector
6. Other

42) Type of Collection `1`
1. Field   4. Peasants store
2. Market   5. Other
3. Seeds store

45) Amount collected `5 0 0`
Units `9`
1. Seeds   7. Ears
2. Grains   8. Cuttings
3. Fruits   9. Grams
4. Plants   10. Kilograms
5. Spikes   11. Measures
6. Tubers   12. Others

43) Age of the sample
(0 - 24) `2` months

46) Herbarium specimen `2`
1. yes   2. no

47) Photograph `2`   1 yes   2 no
Number of roll
Number of shot

IX. Associated collections

	Sheet Number	Accession number	Type of Association
48)	1 3 3 3		3
49)	1 3 4 0		4
50)	1 3 4 1		1
51)			

Types of Association
1. Multiple samples due to heterogenity
2. Main crop
3. Crop associated to this collection
4. Weed of this collection
5. Ecosystem
6. Other

X. Supplemental information

52) Notes

53) Name of the collector `D . Q U E R O L`

54) Name of the taxonomic identifier `D . Q U E R O L`

Notes

LIST OF CODES FOR COUNTRIES AND TERITORIES BY ALPHABETIC ORDER

AFG Afghanistan
ALB Albania
DDR German Democratic Republic
DEU Germany, Federal Republic of
DZA Algeria
AND Andorra
AGO Angola, Peoples Republic of
ANT Netherland Antilles
SAU Saudi Arabia
ARG Argentina
AUS Australia
AUT Austria
BHS Bahamas
BHR Bahrain
BGD Bangladesh
BRB Barbados
BEL Belgium
BLZ Belize
BEN Benin
BMU Bermuda
BTN Bhutan
BUR Burma
BOL Bolivia
BWA Botswana
BRA Brazil
BRN Brunei
BGR Bulgaria, Peoples Republic
HVO Burkina Faso
BDI Burundi
CPV Cape Verde
CMR Cameroon
CAN Canada

TCD Chad
CSK Czechoslovakia, Socialist Republic
CHL Chile
CHN China
CYP Cyprus
COL Colombia
COM Comoros
COG Congo
PRK Korea Democratic People's Republic
KOR Korea, Republic of
CRI Costa Rica
CIV Cote d' Ivoire
CUB Cuba
DNK Denmark
DJI Djibouti
DMA Dominica
TMT East Timor, Peoples Repubic of
ECU Ecuador
EGY Egypt
SLV El Salvador
ARE United Arab Emirates
ESP Spain
USA United States of America
ETH Ethiopia
FJI Fiji
PHL Philippines
FIN Finland
FRA France
GAB Gabon
GMB Gambia
GHA Ghana
GIB Gibraltar
GRD Grenada

GRC Greece
GTM Guatemala
GIN Guinea
GNQ Equatorial Guinea
GNB Guinea-Bissau
GUY Guyana
HTI Haiti
HND Honduras
HKG Hong Kong
HUN Hungary
IND India
IDN Indonesia
IRN Iran
IRQ Iraq
IRL Ireland
NIU Niue
ISL Iceland
CYM Cayman Islands
CTE Canton and Enderbury
     Islands
COK Cook Islands
FRO Faeroe Islands
SLB Solomon Islands
TCA Turks and Caicos Islands
VGB British Virgin Islands
WLS Wallis and Futuna Islands
ISR Israel
ITA Italy
LBY Libyan Arab Jamahiriya
JAM Jamaica
JPN Japan
JOR Jordan
KHM Kampuchea, Democratic
KEN Kenya
KIR Kiribati
KWT Kuwait
LSO Lesotho
LBN Lebanon
LBR Liberia

LIE Liechtenstein
LUX Luxemburg
MAC Macau
MDG Madagaskar
MYS Malaysia
MWI Malawi
MDV Maldives
MLI Mali
MLT Malta
FLK Malvinas
MAR Morocco
MUS Mauritius
MRT Mauritania
MEX Mexico
MCO Monaco
MNG Mongolia
MSR Montserrat
MOZ Mozambique, Peoples
     Republic of
NAM Namibia
NRU Nauru
NPL Nepal
NIC Nicaragua
NER Niger
NGA Nigeria
NOR Norway
NCL New Caledonia
NZL New Zealand
OMN Oman
NLD Netherlands
PAK Pakistan
PAN Panama
PNG Papua New Guinea
PRY Paraguay
PER Peru
PYF French Polynesia
POL Poland, Peoples Republic
     of
PRT Portugal

PRI	Puerto Rico	TTO	Trinidad and Tobago
QAT	Qatar	TUN	Tunisia
GBR	United Kingdom	TUR	Turkey
SYR	Syrian Arab Republic	TUV	Tuvalu
CAF	Central African Republic	UGA	Uganda
LAO	Lao People's Democratic Republic	SUN	Union of Soviet Socialist Republics
DOM	Dominican Republic	URY	Uruguay
ROM	Romania	VUT	Vanuatu
RWA	Rwanda	VEN	Venezuela
WSM	Samoa	VNM	Viet Nam, Democratic Republic of
ASM	American Samoa		
SMR	San Marino	YEM	Yemen
SPM	Saint Pierre and Miquelon	YMD	Yemen Democratic Republic
VCT	Saint Vincent and the Grenadines	YUG	Yugoslavia
SHN	Saint Helena	ZAR	Zaire
LCA	Saint Lucia	ZMB	Zambia
STP	Sao Tome e Principe	ZWE	Zimbabwe
SEN	Senegal		
SYC	Seychelles		
SLE	Sierra Leone		
SGP	Singapore		
SOM	Somalia		
LKA	Sri Lanka		
SDN	Sudan		
ZAF	South Africa		
SWE	Sweden		
CHE	Switzerland		
SUR	Suriname		
SWZ	Swaziland		
THA	Thailand		
TWA	Taiwan, Province of		
TZA	Tanzania, United Republic of		
IOT	British Indian Ocean Territory		
TGO	Togo		
TON	Tonga		

Appendix III

Published descriptor lists
(by crop)

The list of references in the following pages is not comprehensive or complete. These are published descriptor lists which are known by the author.
It is recommended to review Chapter VII in order to design descriptor lists which will be suited to the users needs.

Abelmoschus,
> Charrier, A., (1984),"Genetic resources of the genus *Abelmoschus med* (Okra)", AGPG:IBPGR/84/194, Roma, 61 pp.

Allium,
> Astley, D., Innes, N.L. and Van der Meer, Q.P., (1982),"Genetic resources of *Allium* species.", AGPG:IBPGR/81/77, Roma, 38 pp.

Arachis,
> IBPGR e ICRISAT, (1985),"Descriptors for groundnut (revised).", IBPGR, Roma, 20 pp.

Armeniaca,
> IBPGR, (1980),"Minimal list of descriptors for Apricot.", AGPE:IBPGR/79/42, Roma, 12 pp.

Avena,
> IBPGR, (1985),"Oat descriptors.", IBPGR, Roma, 21 pp.

Beta,
> IBPGR, (1980),"Descriptors for Beets.", AGP:IBPGR/80/61, Roma, 14 pp.

Cajanus,
> IBPGR, (1981),"Descriptors for Pigeonpea.", AGP:IBPGR/80/74, Roma, 15 pp.

Cicer,
> IBPGR, ICARDA e ICRISAT, (1985),"Chickpea descriptors.", AGPG:IBPGR/85/35, Roma, 15 pp.

Cocos,
> IBPGR, (1978),"Coconut genetic Resources", AGPE:IBPGR/78/4, Roma, 24 pp.

Coffea,
    IBPGR, (1980),"Coffee genetic resources.", AGP:IBPGR/80/3,
    Roma, 14 pp.
Colocasia,
    IBPGR, (1980),"Descriptors for *Colocasia.*", AGPE:IBPGR/79/52,
    Roma, 16 pp.
Dioscorea,
    IBPGR, (1980),"Descriptors for Yam (*Dioscorea sp.*).",
    AGPE:IBPGR/79/53, Roma, 20 pp.
Echinochloa,
    IBPGR, (1983),"*Echinochloa* millet descriptors.", AGPG:IBPGR/
    82/77, Roma, 17 pp.
Glycine,
    IBPGR, (1984),"Descriptors for soyabean.", AGPG:IBPGR/84/
    183, Roma, 38 pp.
Gossipium,
    IBPGR, (1985),"Cotton descriptors (revised)", IBPGR, Roma, 17
    pp.
Gossipium,
    IBPGR, (1980),"Descriptors for Cotton species.", AGP:IBPGR/
    80/10, Roma, 18 pp.
Helianthus,
    IBPGR, (1985),"Descriptors for cultivated and wild sunflower.",
    AGPG:IBPGR/85/54, Roma, 33 pp.
Hordeum,
    IBPGR, (1982),"Barley descriptors.", AGPG:IBPGR/82/49, Roma,
    14 pp.
Ipomoea,
    IBPGR, (1981),"Genetic resources of Sweet Potato.",
    AGP:IBPGR/80/63, Roma, 30 pp.
Lens spp.,
    IBPGR e ICARDA, (1985),"Lentil descriptors", AGP:IBPGR/85/
    117, Roma, 15 pp.
Lupinus,
    IBPGR, (1981),"Descriptores de lupinos.", AGP:IBPGR/80/48,
    Roma, 68 pp.
Malus spp.,
    IBPGR, (1982),"Descriptor list for apple (*Malus*)", AGPG:IBPGR/
    82/71, Roma, 46 pp.
Manihot spp.,
    Gulick, P., Hershey, C. and Esquinas Alcazar, J., (1983),"Genetic
    resources of *Cassava* and wild relatives", AGPG:IBPGR/82/111,
    Rome, June 1983*

Musa,
> IBPGR, (1978),"Genetic resources of Bananas and Plantains.", AGPE:IBPGR/77/19, Roma, 20 pp.

Oryza sativa L.,
> IRRI, (1980),"Descriptors for Rice (*Oryza sativa L.*).", International Rice Research Institute, Manila, 21 pp.

Oxalis,
> IBPGR, (1982),"Descriptores de oca.", AGP:IBPGR/82/73, Roma, 23 pp.

Panicum,
> IBPGR, (1985),"Descriptors for *Panicum miliaceum* and *P. sumatrense.*", IBPGR, Roma, 14 pp.

Paspalum scrobicula.,
> IBPGR, (1983),"Descriptors for kodo Millet (*Paspalum scrobiculatum*)", AGPG:IBPGR/82/76, Roma

Pennisetum americanum,
> IBPGR e ICRISAT, (1981),"Descriptors for Pearl millet.", AGP:IBPGR/80/31, Roma, 34 pp.

Phaseolus,
> IBPGR, (1985),"*Phaseolus acutifolius* descriptors.", AGPG:IBPGR/85/31, Roma, 26 pp.

Phaseolus lunatus,
> IBPGR, (1982),"Lima Bean descriptors", IBPGR/82/5

Phaseolus vulgaris,
> IBPGR, (1982),"Descriptors for *Phaseolus vulgaris*", IBPGR/81/1, Roma, 32 pp.

Psophocarpus,
> IBPGR, (1982),"Revised winged bean descriptors.", AGPG:IBPGR/81/78, Roma, 17 pp.

Prunus,
> IBPGR, (1981),"Almond descriptors.", AGP:IBPGR/80/88, Roma, 21 pp.

Psophocarpus,
> IBPGR, (1979),"Descriptors for the Winged Bean.", AGPE:IBPGR/79/5, Roma, 24 pp.

Quinua,
> IBPGR, (1981),"Descriptores de quinua", AGP:IBPGR/81/104, Roma, 18 pp.

Saccharum,
> IBPGR, (1982),"Genetic resources of sugarcane.", AGPG:IBPGR/81/74, Roma, 19 pp.

Secale,
> IBPGR, (1985),"Descriptors for rye and triticale.", IBPGR, Roma,

13 pp.

Setaria,

IBPGR, *(1985),"Descriptors for Setaria italica* and *S. pumila.",* IBPGR, Roma, 18 pp.

Sorghum,

IBPGR e ICRISAT, (1984),"Revised *Sorghum* descriptors.", AGPG:IBPGR/84/142, Roma, 36 pp.

Theobroma,

IBPGR, (1981),"Genetic resources of Cocoa.", AGP:IBPGR/80/ 56, Roma, 25 pp.

Theobroma,

Engels, J.M.M., Bartley, G.G.C. y Enriquez, G.A., (1980),"Cocoa descriptors, their states and modus operandi.", Turrialba 30:209-218.

Triticum,

IBPGR and CEC, (1985),"Revised descriptor list for wheat (*Triticum spp.*)", AGPG:IBPGR/85/210, Roma, 12 pp.

Triticum,

IBPGR, (1981),"Revised descriptors for wheat.", AGP:IBPGR/ 81/51, Roma, 12 pp.

Triticum,

Anonymous, (1980),"Descriptores para trigo.", The plant gene resources of Canada, 7 pp.

Tropical fruits,

IBPGR, (1980),"Revised descriptor list for tropical fruits.", AGP:IBPGR/80/54, Roma, 11 pp.

Vicia,

IBPGR e ICARDA, (1985),"Faba bean descriptors.", AGPG:IBPGR/85/116, Roma, 19 pp.

Vigna,

IBPGR, (1985),"Descriptors for *Vigna mungo* and *V. radiata* (Revised)", IBPGR, Roma, 23 pp.

Vigna,

IBPGR, (1985),"Descriptors for *Vigna aconitifolia* and *V. trilobata.*", AGPG:IBPGR/85/34, Roma, 39 pp.

Vigna radiata,

IBPGR, (1980f),"Descriptors for Mung Bean.", AGP:IBPGR/80/ 35, Roma, 18 pp.

Vitis,

IBPGR, (1982),"Descriptors for grape.", AGP:IBPGR/83/154, Roma, 93 pp.

Zea,

IBPGR, (1980),"Maize descriptors.", AGP:IBPGR/80/94, Roma, 9 pp.

Appendix IV

Procedures to obtain genetic resource samples

Whoever wants material from a genebank should:

1. Write a letter to the genebank where he or she knows or assumes the material needed exists, specifying the characteristics of what material is needed, e.g. "10 samples of red beans (*Phaseolus vulgaris*) collected between 0 and 15 degrees North and South of the equator, between 100 and 500 m above sea level".

2. Ensure the appropiate transfer procedures with the genebank, especially in the case of vegetatively reproduced crops, including quarantine and customs clearances.

Two factors will determine the handing out of the material (if no political or economic reasons are behind). On one hand, the number of different samples requested and on the other the amount of seeds requested for each sample. Most small genebanks do not have the resources or the personnel to handle large requests ("Please send me a copy of each of your 3000 maize accessions"), which are rarely justified because they are not used. As to sample size, the user should not expect large seed samples, even less so in the case of vegetative material. Seeds are generally sent in 100-seed envelopes and one should therefore generally plan a first multiplication planting before the material is actually used in evaluations or other experiments.

Some useful addresses are:

IBPGR
(Dr. J.Trevor Williams, Executive Secretary)
International Board for Plant Genetic Resources.
Via delle Terme di Caracalla
00100 Roma, Italy
(Source of information on the political and technical position of IBPGR.

You may ask for IBPGR publications, which are distributed free of charge.)

FAO Plant Genetic Resources Comission
(Dr. José Esquinas Alcazar, Technical Secretary)
FAO
Via delle Terme di Caracalla
00100 Roma, Italy
(Source of information within FAO on the technical issues)

Vavilov Plant Production Institut
(Dr. V.F. Dorofeev)
44 Herzen Street
Leningrado
USSR
(Main genebank in the Soviet Union)

International Genetic Resources Program
Pat Mooney
RRI (Beresford)
Brandon, Manitoba R7A 5Y1
Canada
(Source of information on the international political situation)

U.S. Department of Agriculture, SEA
Plant Introduction of Germplasm Resources Laboratory
(Dr. George White)
Beltsville, Maryland 20705
USA
(Entry and exit point of most accesions in the USA. Source of material.)

Seeds Action Network (SAN)
(Henk Hobbelink)
Apartado 23398
Barcelona 08080
SPAIN
(Network of NGO and independent workers on Seeds and Genetic Resources. Publishes "The Seedling".)

The addresses of other genebanks and information on the type of genetic resources they store can be found in the following publications available from IBPGR:

Ayad, G. and Murthi Anishetty, N., (1980)
  "Directory of germplasm collections. I. Food Legumes.", AGP: IBPGR/80/45, Roma 22 pp.
Ayad, G., Toll, J. and Esquinas Alcazar, J.T., (1980)
  "Directory of germplasm collections. III. Cereals. 2. Maize", IBPGR/80/90. Roma 23 pp.
Ayad, G., Toll, J. and Williams, J.T., (1980)
  "Directory of germplasm collections. III. Cereals. 1. Wheat", AGP: IBPGR/80/89. Roma 28 pp.
Damania, A.B. and Williams, J.T., (1980)
  "Directory of germplasm collections. II. Root crops.", AGP: IBPGR/80/49. Roma 54 p.p,
Ellis Davies, W. and McLean, B.T., (1984)
  "Directory of germplasm collections. VII. Forages (grasses, legumes, etc.).", AGPG:IBPGR/83/90, Roma, 43 pp.
Gulick, P. and van Sloten, D.H., (1984)
  "Directory of germplasm collections. VI. Tropical and subtropical fruits and tree nuts.", AGPG:IBPGR/84/85, Roma, 191 pp.
Hawkes, E., (1972)
  "European and regional gene banks", Proceedings of a conference on European and Regional Gene Banks, IZMIR, Turkey, 10-15 April 1972, Edited by Hankes and Langles
Toll, J. and van Sloten, D.H., (1982)
  "Directory of germplasm collections. IV.Vegetables.", AGP:IBPGR/82/1, Roma, 187 pp.
Toll, J., Ayad, G. and Witcombe, W., (1982)
  "Directory of germplasm collections. III. Cereals. 5. Barley", AGP: IBPGR/81/989, Roma, 26 pp.
Toll, J., Murthi Anishetty, N. and Ayad, G., (1980)
  "Directory of germplasm collections. III. Cereals. 3. Rice.", AGP:IBPGR/80/109, Roma, 20 pp.
Toll, J., Murthi Anishetty, N. and Ayad, G., (1981)
  "Directory of germplasm collections. III. Cereals. 4. Sorghum and Millets.", AGP:IBPGR/81/55, Roma, 37 pp.
Williams, J.T. and Damania, A.B., (1981)
  "Directory of germplasm collections. V. Industrial crops 1. Cacao, coconut, pepper, sugarcane and tea.", AGP:IBPGR/81/97, Roma, 50 pp.

Appendix V
GLOSSARY

Accesion
A sample (variety, strain, cultivar, or a bulk population) which enters
a genetic ressouces center for conservation or use.

Agar
Gel produced from marine algae which is used as support environment in tissue culture.

Allele
One of an alternate form of a gene, located in a certain position (locus)
on a particular chromosome or linkage group. When the alternates
exceed two, the alleles form a multiple allelic series.

Allogamous plants
Cross-fertilized plants.

Annual Plants
A plant which completes its life span from seed to seed within a single
year or season.

Anther
Upper part of the stamen which contains the pollen.

Anthesis
The period, in a flower, when the anthers are fully ripe.

Asexual reproduction
Reproduction which does not involve the union of gametes (fertilization) and which generally occurs through the division of vegetative
cells.

Autogamous Plants
Plants which self-fertilise and do not cross with other plants of the
same species.

GENETIC RESOURCES

Biennial Plants
Plants that take two years to complete their life-cycle.

Characterization
The measurement of all characters with high inheritance and which express in all environments. The curator will insure that they be easily obtained, generally during multiplication and regeneration of an accession.

Chromosomal aberrations
In genetics, a change in the normal number of chromosomes, their break with incomplete repair or the loss of a chromosome segment.

Chromosomes
Structural units of the nucleus which carry genes in a linear order, found in homologous pairs in somatic cells of plants. Chromosomes house the genetic information, provide mechanisms for releasing and regulating the transmission of this information during development according to a precise programme.

Clone
The vegetative progeny of a common ancestor. Since they are derived from a single plant, they are therefore of the same genotype, as in the case of bananas and potatoes.

Collecting Trip
Field trip to get wild and cultivated genetic variability which cannot be obtained in existing collections.

Collection Garden or Clonal Garden
Collection in the field of vegetatively reproduced crops. Also used to maintain outstanding genetic combinations of seed reproduced crops, e.g. Fruit trees.

Collection, Base or Long-term
Genetic ressources collection kept for long term conservation, generally seeds stored below -15 C with a very low humidity contents.

Collection, Medium-term
Genetic ressources collection to be kept at least for 20 years without regeneration, like in the case of orthodox seeds stored at -4 C at 6% water content.

Collection, Working or short-term
Genetic ressources collection of which the samples are not expected to survive beyond 5 years without regeneration.

Continuous variation
See: Quantitative characters

Cryopreservation
Storage of tissues and organisms at ultra-low temperatures, generally liquid nitrogen (-196 C).

Cryoprotectants
Substances used to protect the tissues from damage due to the formation of ice crystals during cryopreservation.

Cultivars
Cultivated varieties. See: Modern Varieties.

Data Base
A collection of information on accessions which includes the descriptors and the associated descriptor states.

Descriptor
The single basis for the description of an item of information. It may assume different values (See also: Descriptor states).

Descriptor list
All the descriptors associated with a plant. It includes passport and other identification data.

Descriptor states
A series of mutually exclusive values for a descriptor in each of its possibilities, or in each of the possible values it may assume.

Dioecious Plants
Refers to species with male and female flowers on separate plants.

Diploid
Organism possessing two complete sets of chromosomes. Generally each of the two parents contributes one set.

Discontinuous variation
See: Qualitative characters.

Dormancy, Seed
State in which certain live seeds do not germinate even under optimum conditions. Dormancy can be due to a series of factors described in the book.

Endogamy
Inbreeding. When an alogamous plant is crossed with itself over various generations, a loss of vigour is observed, which is called endogamic depression.

Gene
Inheritance unit composed of a chain of Deoxi-ribonucleic Acid (DNA), generally found in a chromosome, which codes the chaining of amino-acids in a specific sequence.

Genetic Drift
Change in the genetic composition of a population, when the number of individuals is reduced below the frequency of certain alleles within it.

Genetics
Science which studies inheritance and its chemical and physiological base.

Genotype
The genetic constitution (the genetic characteristics) of an individual plant or other organism.

Germination
Biological process which eventually leads to the development of a plantlet starting from a seed. The emergence of a radicle is the first visible sign, but germination starts from the first seed moistening proceses.

Germination Test
Test on seed samples to determine the percentage of seeds with germination capability. See also: Germination.

Germplasm
The sum total of the genetic material in a plant.

Germplasm- or Gene-Bank
Concept which includes cold-rooms for the storage of seeds, air-conditioned areas for the storage of plant pieces or in-vitro plantlets and collection gardens for the storage of grown plants.

Grid
In the case of a genetic resources collection, the division of a geographic area into squares of uniform size. In each square, samples should be taken.

Haploid
Cell with only one set of chromosomes per nucleus, as in the case of pollen spores and gametes of higher plants.

Heterogeneous sample or population
Non -uniform sample or population. In Genetic Resources it corresponds to typical populations of traditional varieties.

Heterozygous
With different alleles on the chromosomes on one or more loci.

Homogeneous sample or population
Uniform sample or population. In genetic resouces it correponds to the populations of modern varieties and to vegetatively reproduced plants.

Homozygous
With the same allele on both chromosomes (or various chromosomes in the case of a polyploid) for one or various genes.

Hybrid seed
Seed from the first generation from a cross between two individuals differing in one or more genes. The hybrid characteristics are lost in the next generation.

Hygroscopic
Which atracts water.

In vitro
In glass. Refers to the establishment of cells and organs in glass vials (sometimes also plastic, metal, etc.). In a wide sense, the use of vials with artificial media for the development of organisms in the laboratory.

Isoenzymes
Different forms of enzymes fulfilling the same function, which are coded by different alleles of one or various genes. They are used to determine, through electrophoresis, whether two accessions have the same alele on a certain gene.

Isolation in seed production
Procedure used to avoid genetic mixtures due to cross-pollination with outside plants of the same species. It is achieved through distance, different planting dates to avoid simmultaneous flowering and through physical barriers.

Locus (plural= loci)
The position occupied by a gene on a chromosome.

Meiosis
Two succesive divisions of the cell nucleus, whereby the diploid cromosome number is reduced to haploid.

Meristem
The growth area with accelerated cell division at the tip of a branch or shoot.

Mitosis
Division process in the cellular nucleus, after which the cells originated have the same constitution as the original cell.

Monoecious
Plant with sexed flowers; male and female flowers are on the same plant, but separated.

Monoploid
See: Haploid.

Mutation
The instantaneous origin of variablity which is inherited. It includes changes in the genes, changes in the chromosome structure and in

certain cases changes in the chromosome number. It may be natural or induced by man.

Pathogen
See: Pests.

Pests
Global concept which includes the following three types of adverse factors:

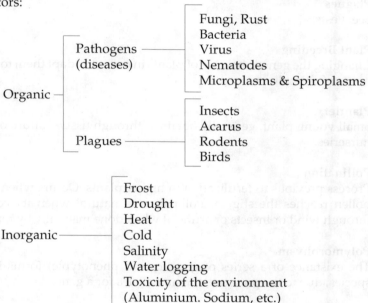

The term pests includes diseases and plagues, and by extension the inorganic causes of plant disfunction.

Phenotype
The external appearance of a plant, as a result of the interaction of its genetic composition (genotype) with the environment.

Photoperiod
Number of hours of light and darkness in a day, which is a factor of latitude and period of the year. It is an essential factor for the flowering of many plant species.

Phylogenetics
Study of the ancestral relationships of species to one another.

Physiological Race
A group of organisms which differentiate themselves from other individuals of the same species only by their physiological or ecological behaviour.

Plagues
See: Pests.

Plant Breeding
Changing the genetic balance of plants in order to adapt them to the needs of agriculture.

Plantlet
Small young plant, generally obtained through tissue culture or in nurseries.

Pollination
Process previous to fertilization in higher plants. Occurs when the pollen reaches the stigma. Pollination is natural when it occurs through wind or insects or artificial when done manually by man.

Polymorphysm
The existance of a series of genetic (and phenotypic) forms in a species, due to the presence of many alleles for a gene.

Polyploid
An organism which the number of chromosome sets is a multiple of the haploid state.

Population
Group of individuals (plant or animals) who share a geographic space and have common traits.

Preservation
The practice which allows to perpetuate a resource.

Progeny
Offspring. All the plants which originate from a given plant.

Qualitative Characters
Characters controlled by one or few genes in which the distinction between the expression of the different alleles is clear cut. There is no continuous expression of these characters (discontinuous variation).

Quantitative Characters
Characters which can be measured numerically and generally correspond to continuous variation. If a character shows continuous variation, classification into discrete categories will be arbitrary.

Regeneration
Planting of a seed sample to produce seeds with a genetic constitution simmilar to the original sample, and which will allow to replace the previously stored seed with healthier ones.

Sample
A part of a population taken to estimate the characteristics of the whole.

Sample, Biased
Sample taken from a population which does not represent it, when visual evidence exists that certain different plant types, with low frequencies, are present. The biased sample allows to maintain interesting plant types. See also: Sample, Random.

Sample, Random
Sample taken from a population to represent it as accurately as possible, including all present forms. See also: Sample, Biased.

Sampling
Collection of variants to represent the range of genetic variability available in a population.

Seed
1. Botanical Seed. In a strict botanical sense it is an embryo with one or two cotyledons, surrounded with a seed cover.
2. Seed. By extension, the term seed is used for everything used to plant in the field, even if it is not botanical seed, as in the case of potatoes and bananas.

Seed viability
Potential germination of a seed under favourable conditions, assuming

the dormancy causing factors were eliminated.

Seeds, Orthodox
Seeds for which the viability period increases in a logarithmic curve as the storage temperature and humidity contents of the seeds are reduced.

Seeds, Recalcitrant
Seeds which do not follow the rules which apply to orthodox seeds, as they quickly loose viability when dryed or stored at low temperatures.

Seeds, Traditional, Bred
See: Varieties.

Species
A taxonomic category. The basic unit in classification.
a) Taxonomic or morphological species concept. The smallest natural populations separated from each other by a distinct discontinuity in the series of biotypes.
b)Biological species concept. Species are groups of interbreeding natural populations that do not produce fertile progenies when crossed with other populations under natural conditions. In a wide sense it is the whole of the plants or population belonging to the species.

Species, Conventional
All those species which have been studied by modern science and which generally are found under modern production processes. This implies that the breeding, cultivation and processing techniques are known, and a national and/or international market is available. See also: Species, Non Conventional.

Species, Introduced
Species which is not native to the area of collection, its center of origin being elsewhere.

Species, Native
Species whose center of origin or domestication is in the area under study. By extension, a species which is used for over 500 years in the area.

Species, Non-conventional
Species on which only the empirical researchers (peasants, medicine men, whitch doctors, etc.) have knowledge on, and the study of which with modern techniques could lead to certain technical conventions. They may be native or traditional species. See also: Species, Conventional.

Species, Wild
Plants which grow normally without man's participation. A special case are those forms which have escaped from cultivation.

Stigma
Upper part of the pistil destined to receive and retain the pollen grains.

Taxonomy
The study of classification.

Taxonomy, Classical
The classification (of plants) based on morphological characters of the reproductive organs.

Taxonomy, Numerical
The classification (of plants) based on the numerical simmilarity of the measured characters and the ordering of these into groups.

Varieties, Bred
See: Varieties, Modern.

Varieties, Modern
Cultivated plants which have been bred to satisfy present consumer requirements, generally of lower nutritional and taste value than traditional varieties, to be cultivated under modern technological processes (High yields while using high levels of fertilizer and pesticides). The term bred-varieties should not be used, as it would exclude the traditional varieties bred over thousands of years by the peasants.

Varieties, Native
See: Species, Native.

Varieties, Primitive
Demeaning term for traditional varieties. See: Varieties, Traditional.

Varieties, Traditional
Varieties used traditionally by peasants in a speciffic area. It includes traditional varieties of native and introduced species. The first bred for thousands of years, the second introduced and adapted to local conditions.

Variety
Group of cultivated plants within a species distinct from another group through one or many characters (morphological, physiological, biochemical or other) and which, when reproduced, maintains the characters which distinguish it.

Viability Test
Test on a seed sample which estimates the percentage of viable seeds. It is used when dormant seeds are expected to be present. See also: Dormancy.

Weed
No universally valid definition of this term is available, as the 'weeds' of one are the crops of others. When man was a gatherer, he differentiated plants as usefull, dangerous and unknown. The 'weed' appeared with agriculture, and more speciffically with monoculture. Weeds could be defined as plants which grow where the peasant or farmer does not want them to grow.